This Book Belongs To:

_____

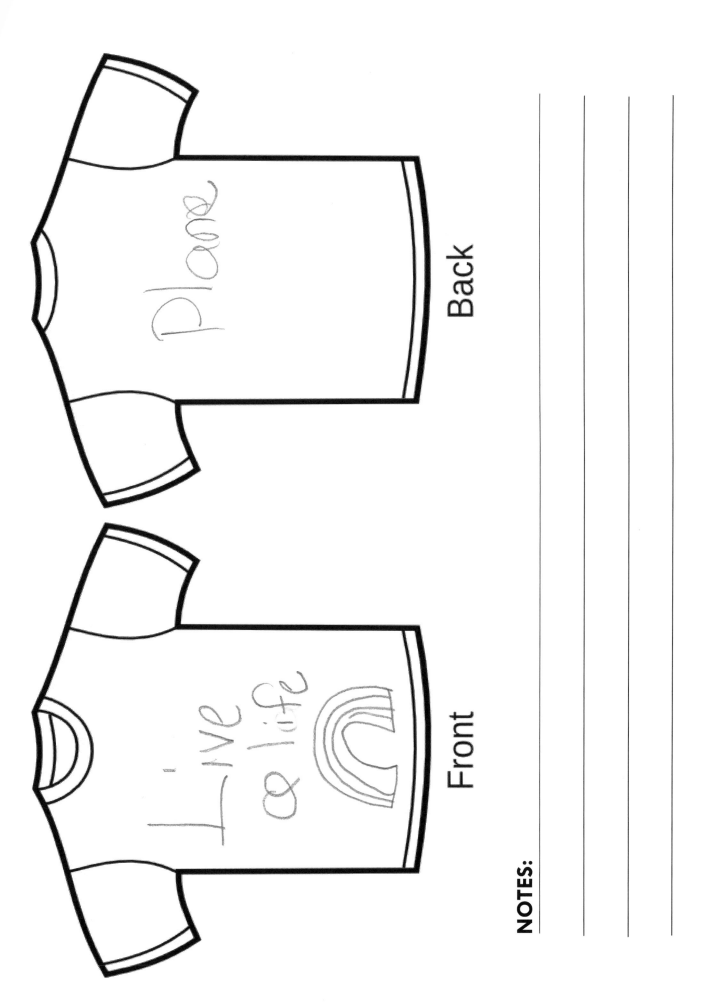

Back

Front

NOTES:

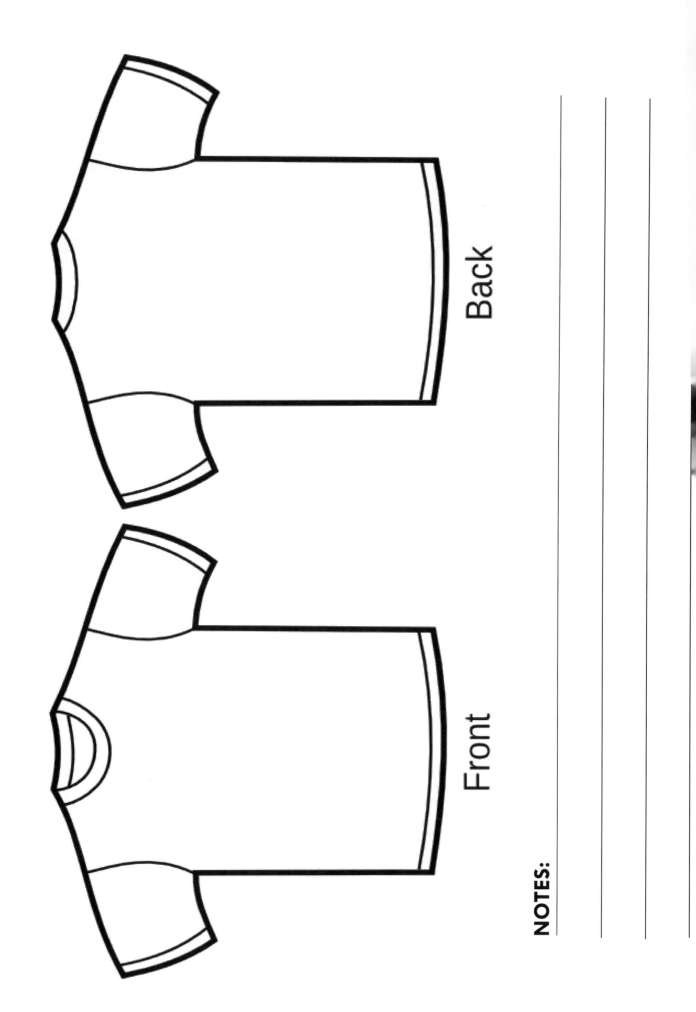

Back

Front

NOTES:

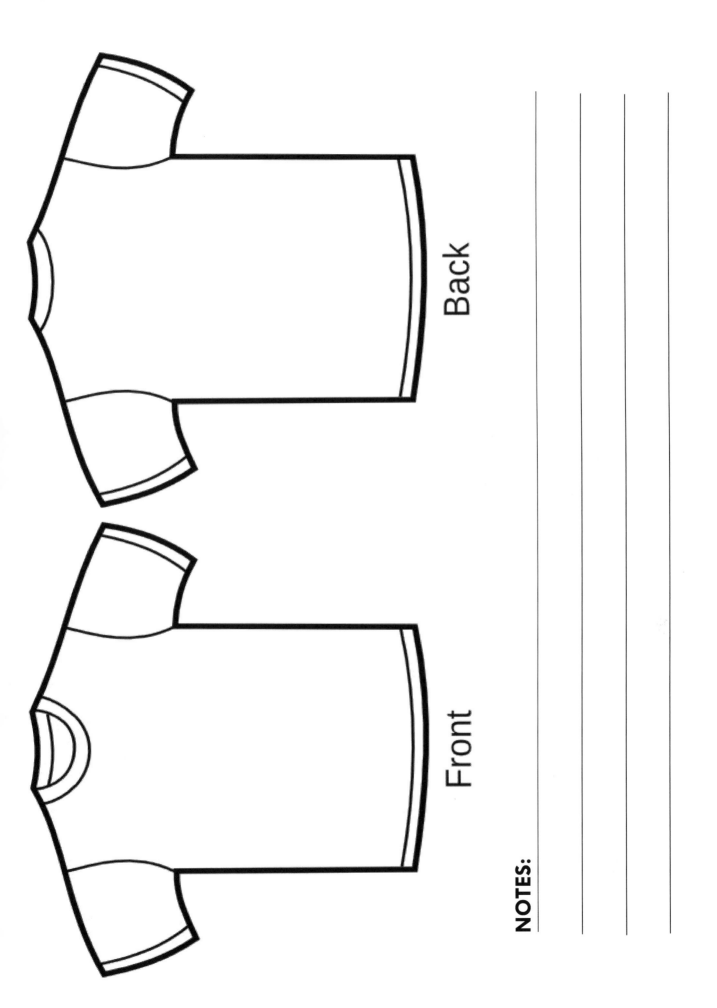

Back

Front

NOTES:

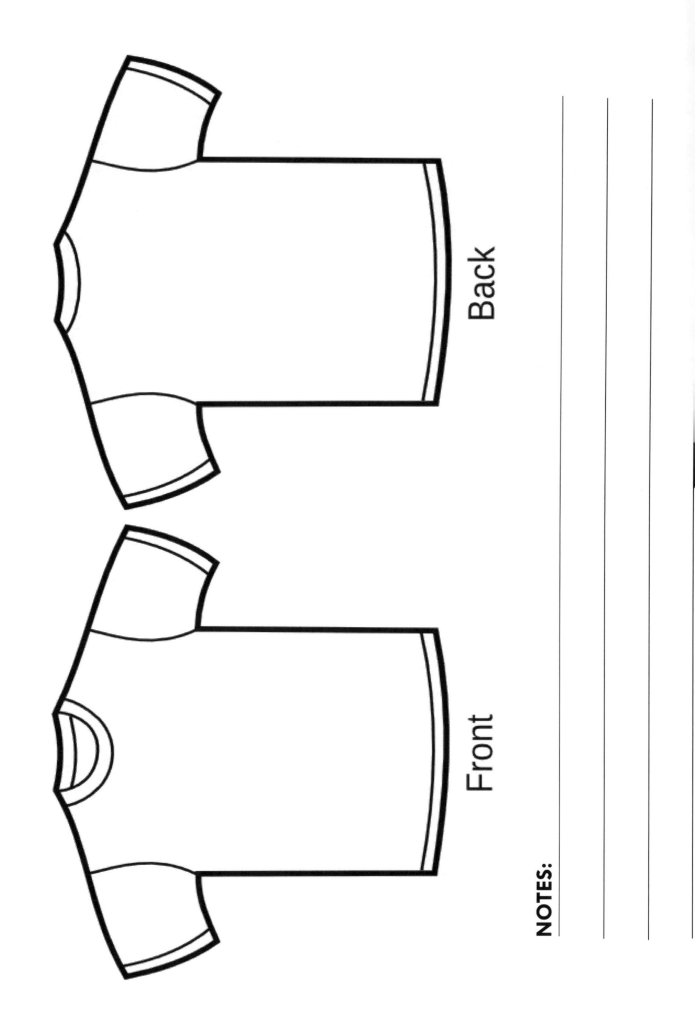

Back

Front

NOTES:

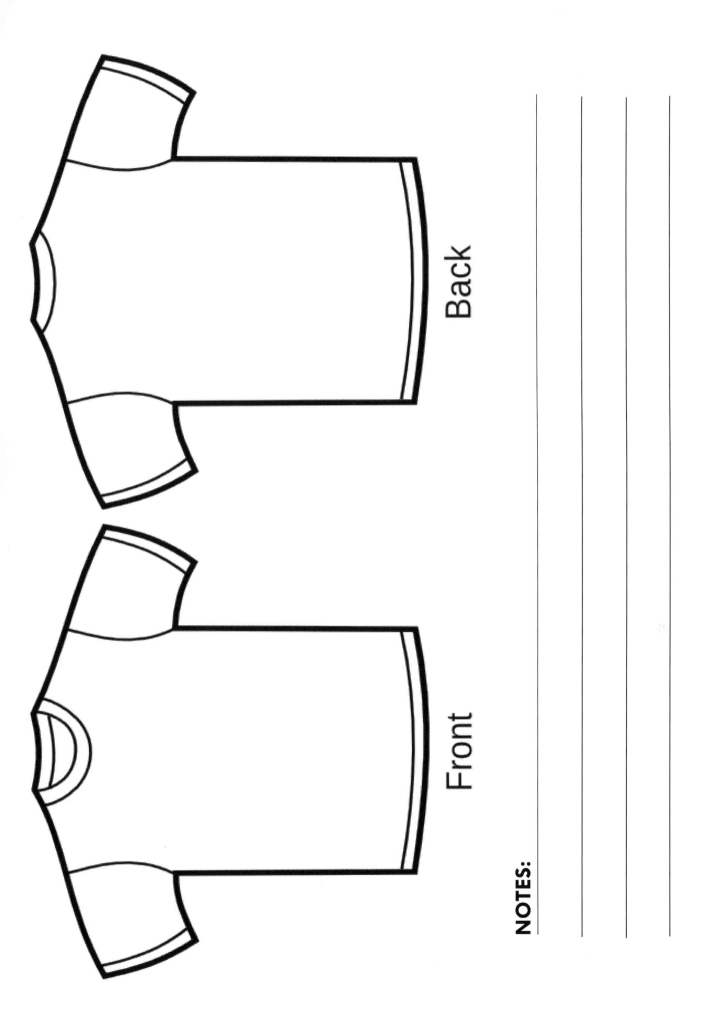

Back

Front

NOTES:

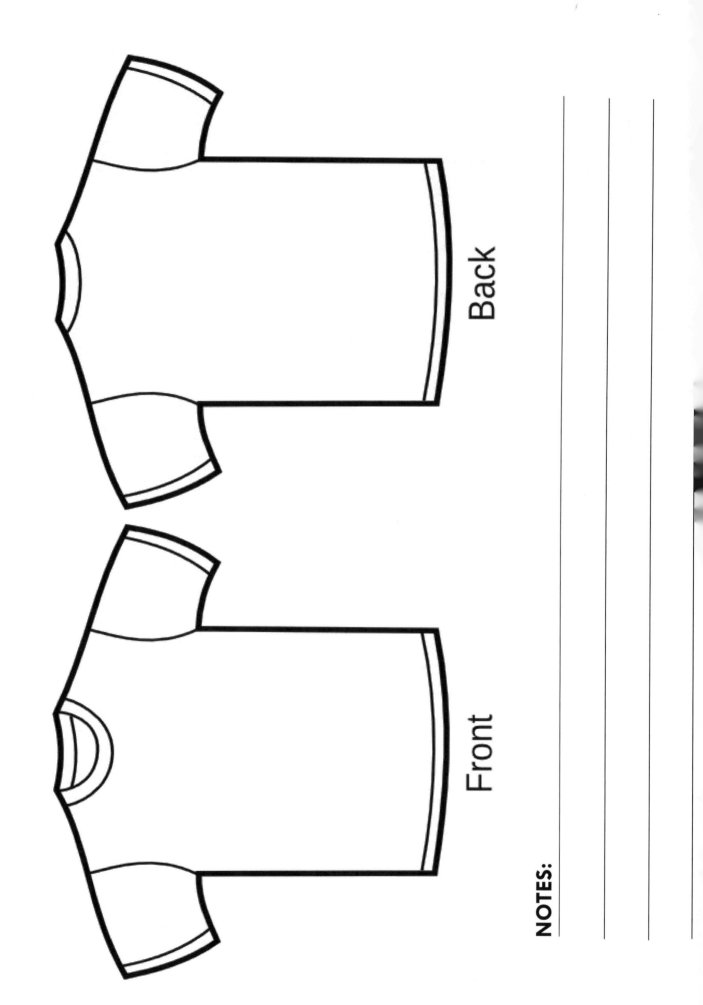

Back

Front

NOTES:

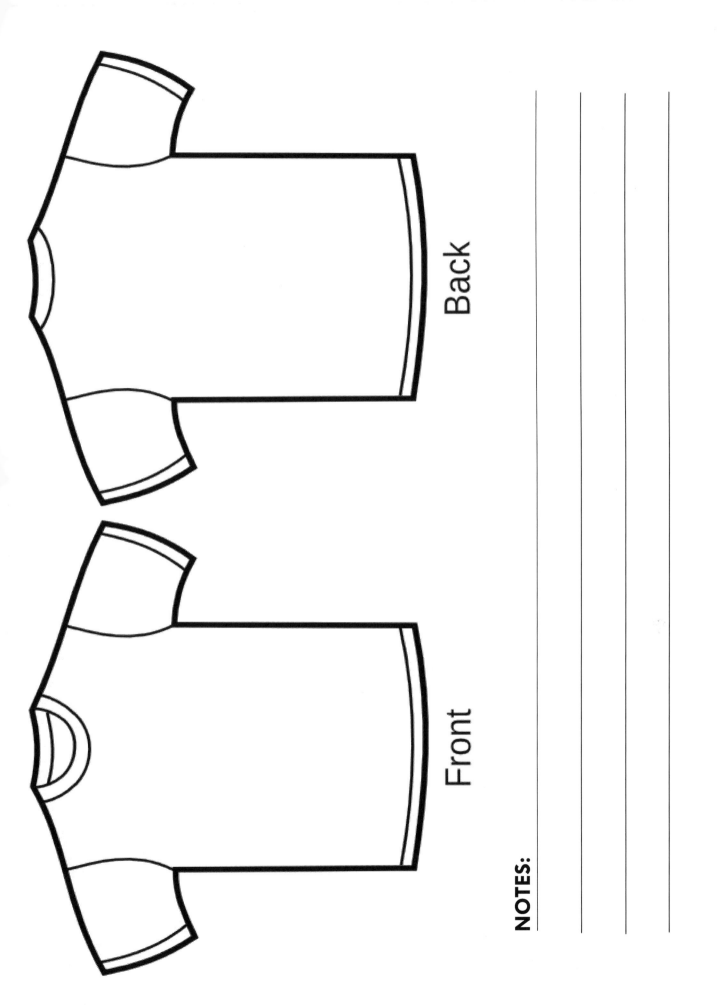

Back

Front

NOTES:

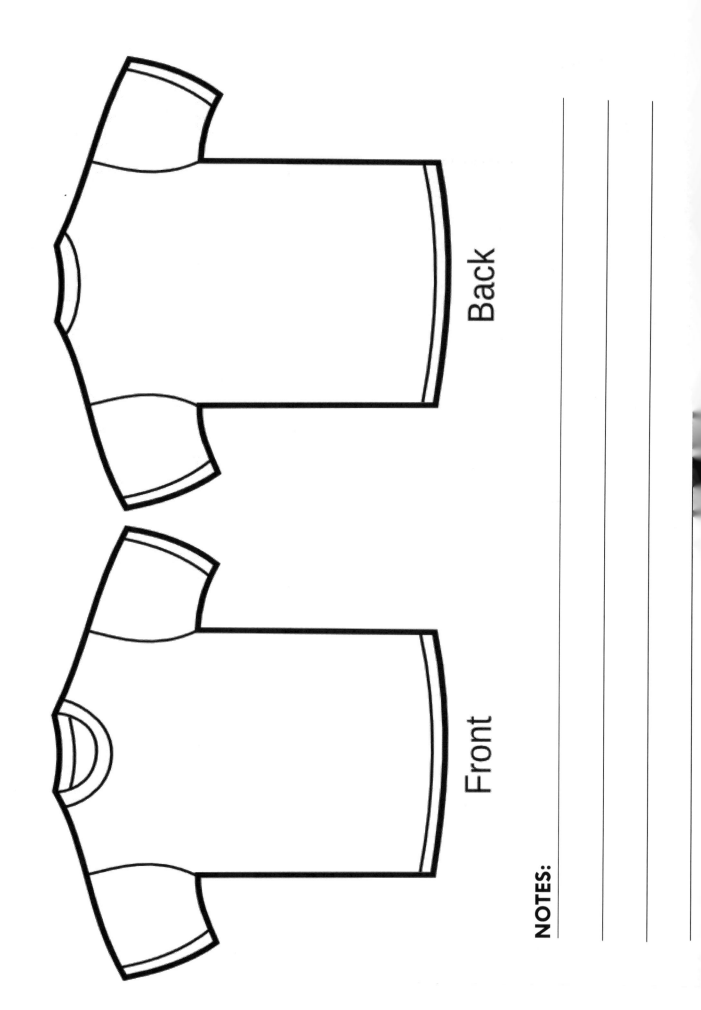

Back

Front

NOTES:

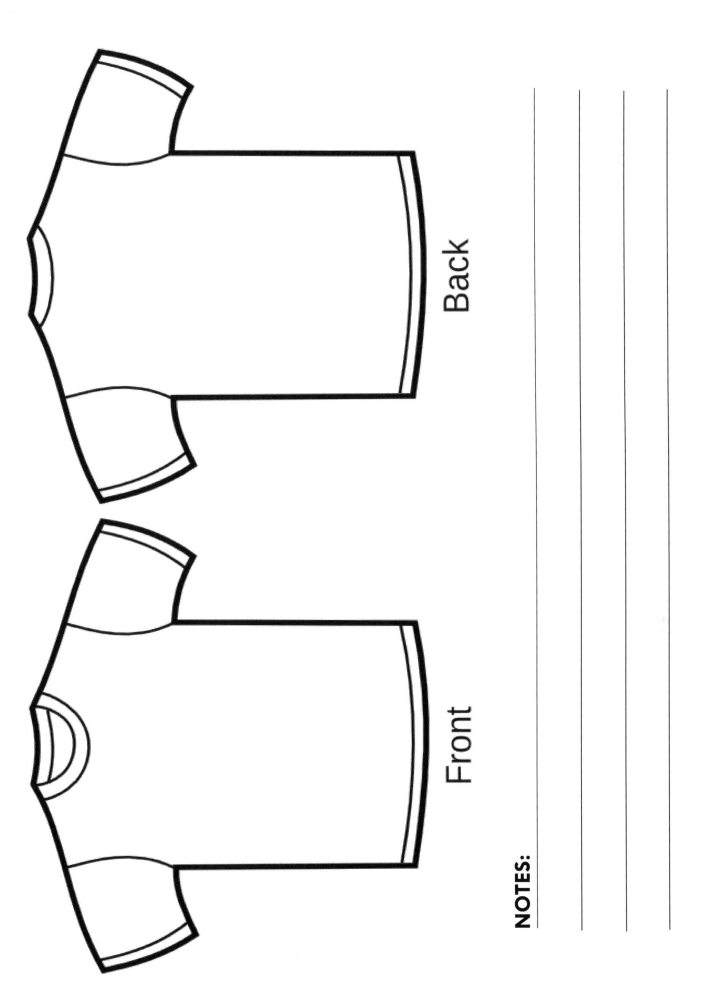

Back

Front

NOTES:

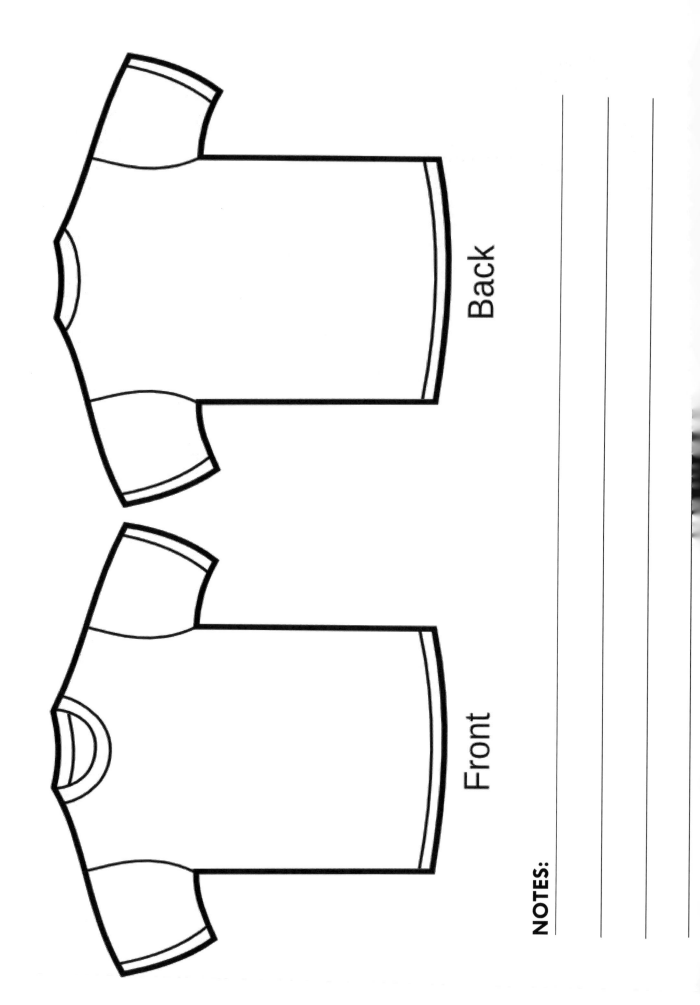

Back

Front

NOTES:

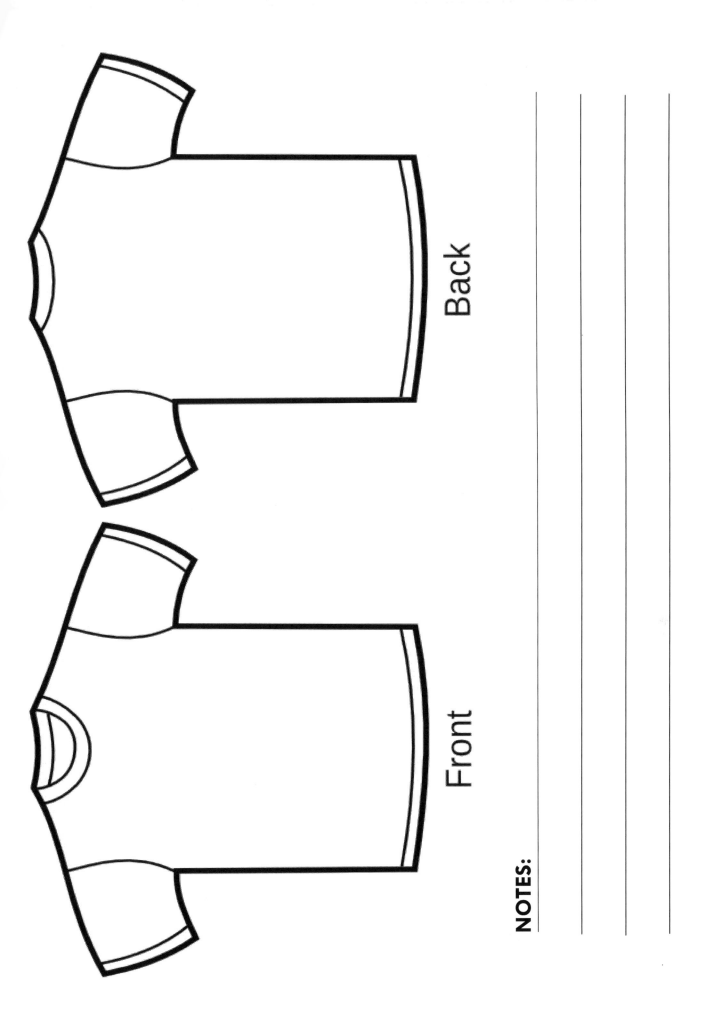

Back

Front

NOTES:

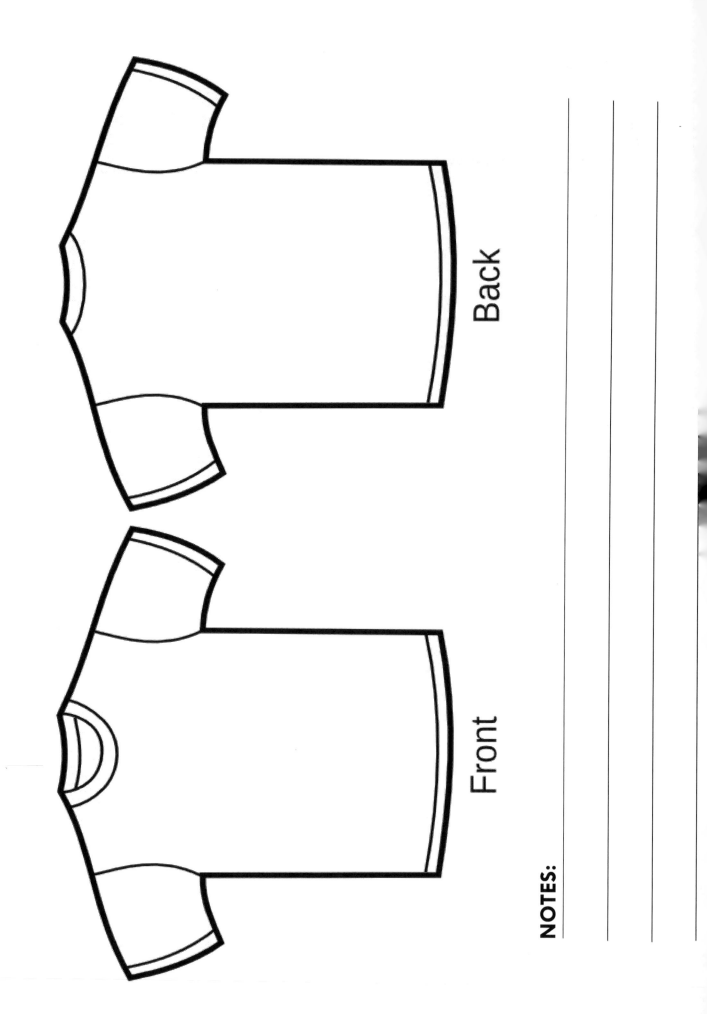

Back

Front

NOTES:

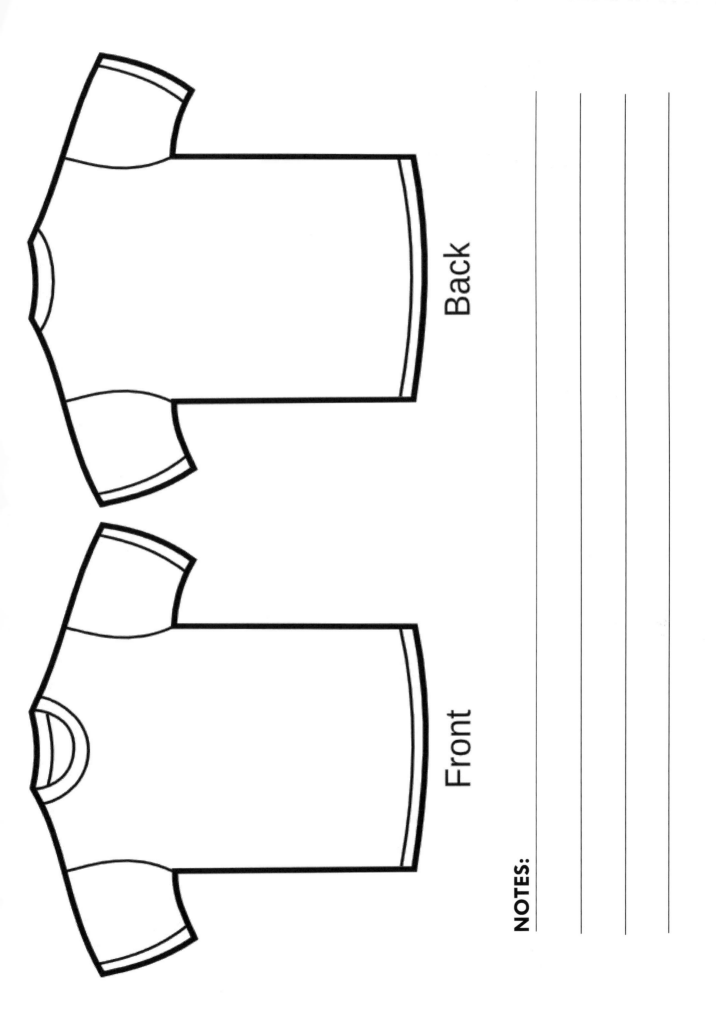

Back

Front

NOTES:

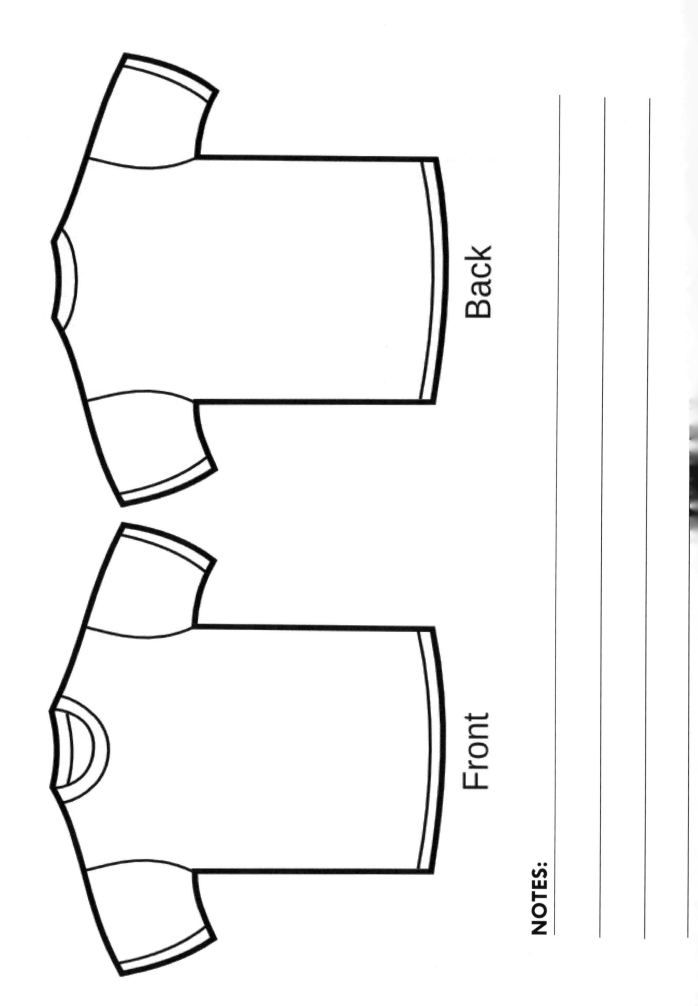

Back

Front

NOTES:

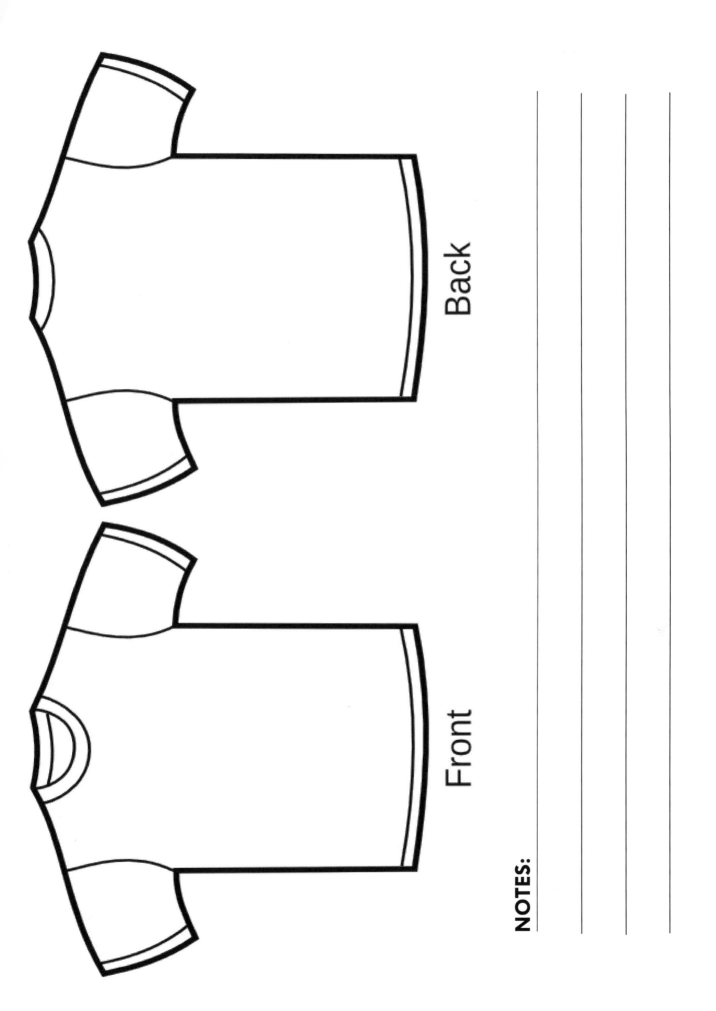

Back

Front

NOTES:

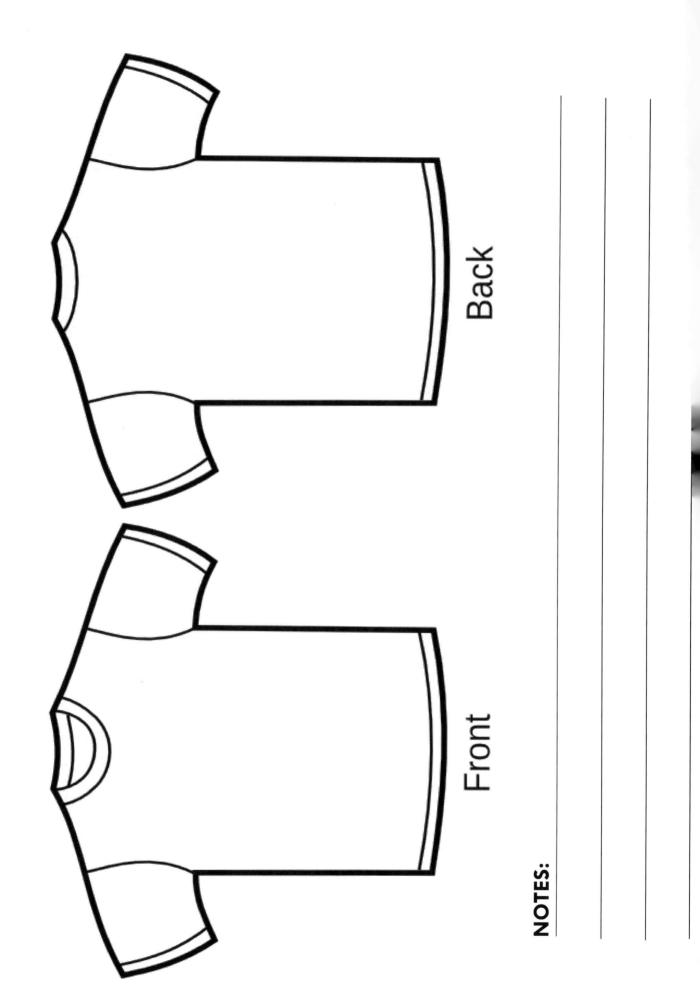

Back

Front

NOTES:

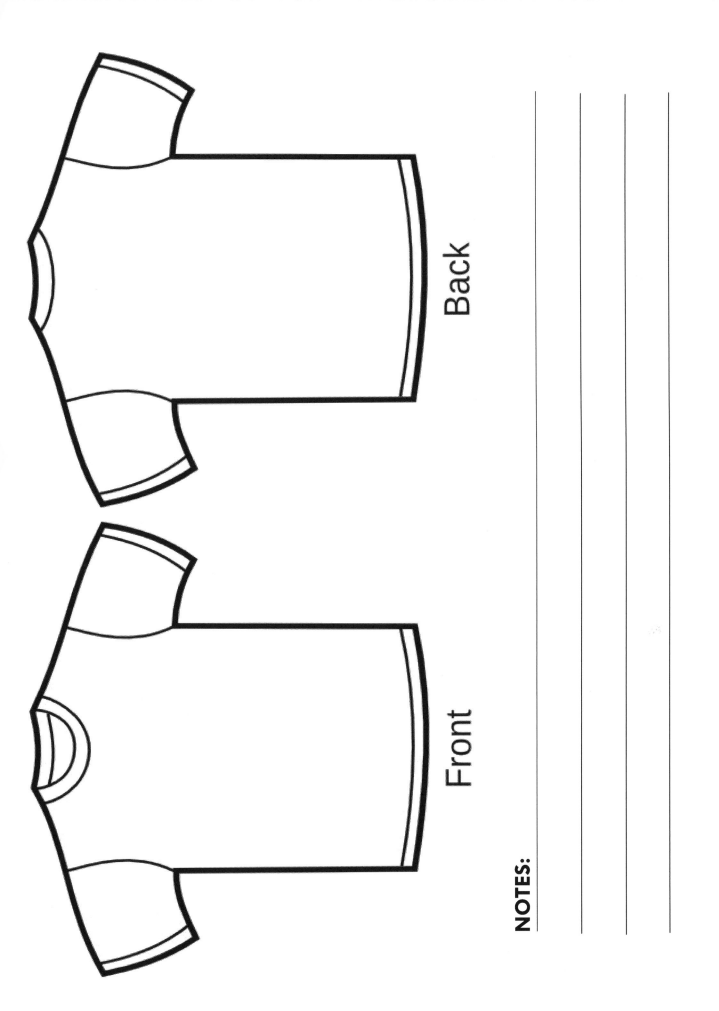

Back

Front

NOTES:

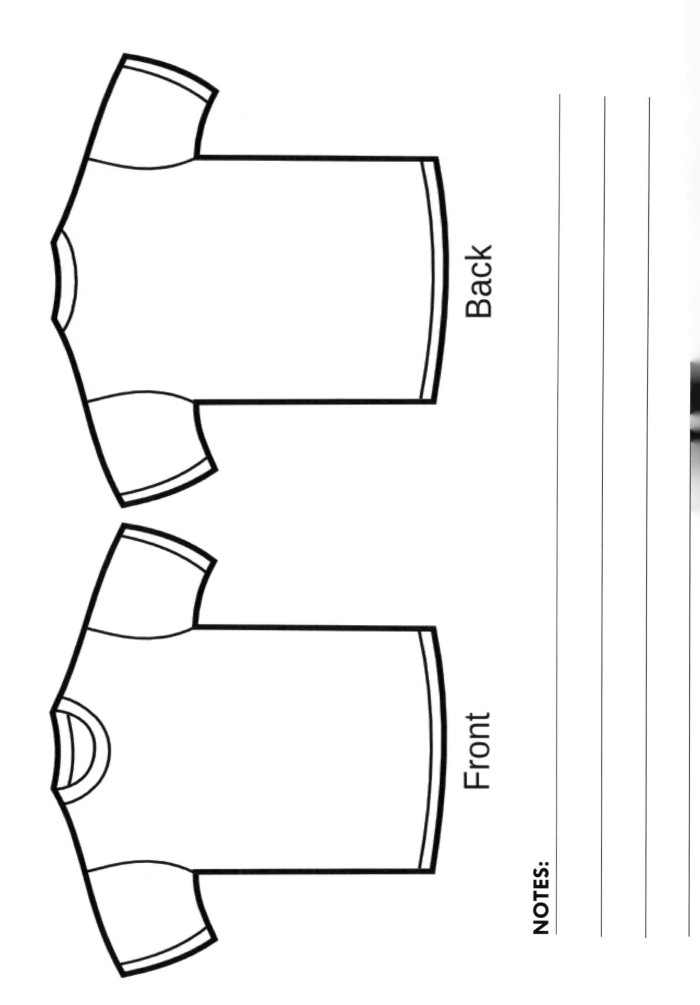

Back

Front

NOTES:

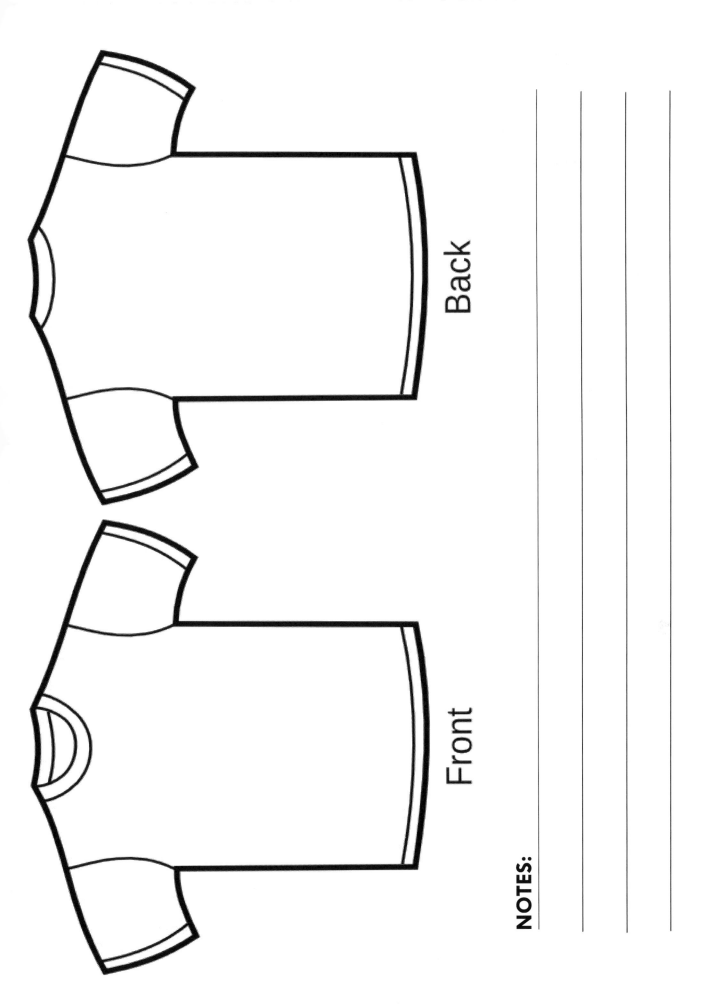

Back

Front

NOTES:

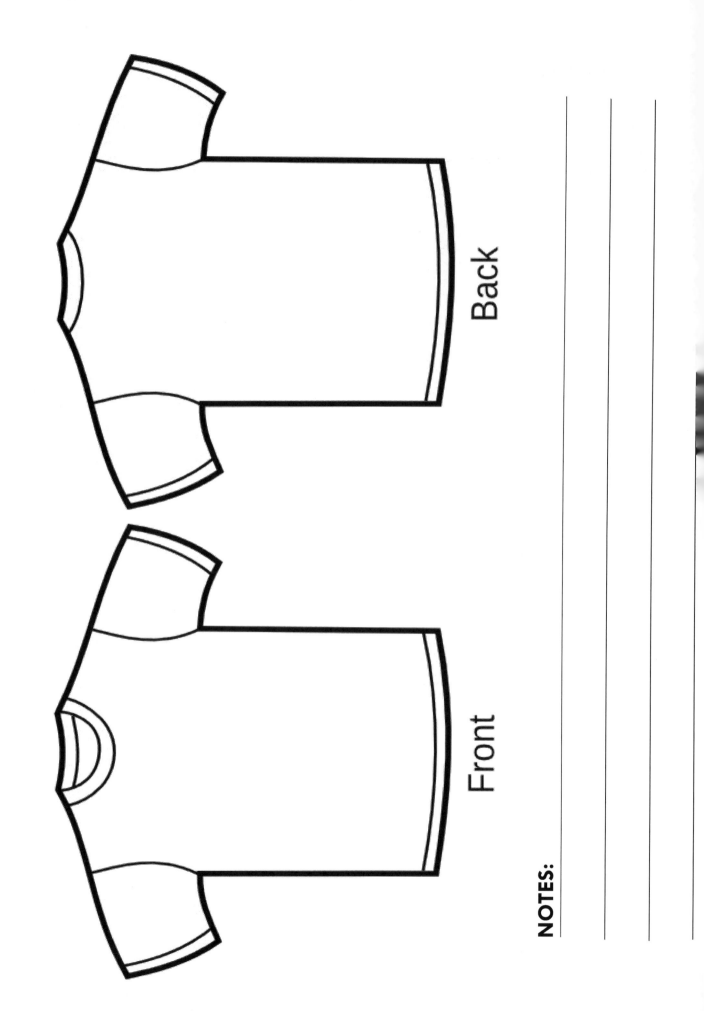

Back

Front

NOTES:

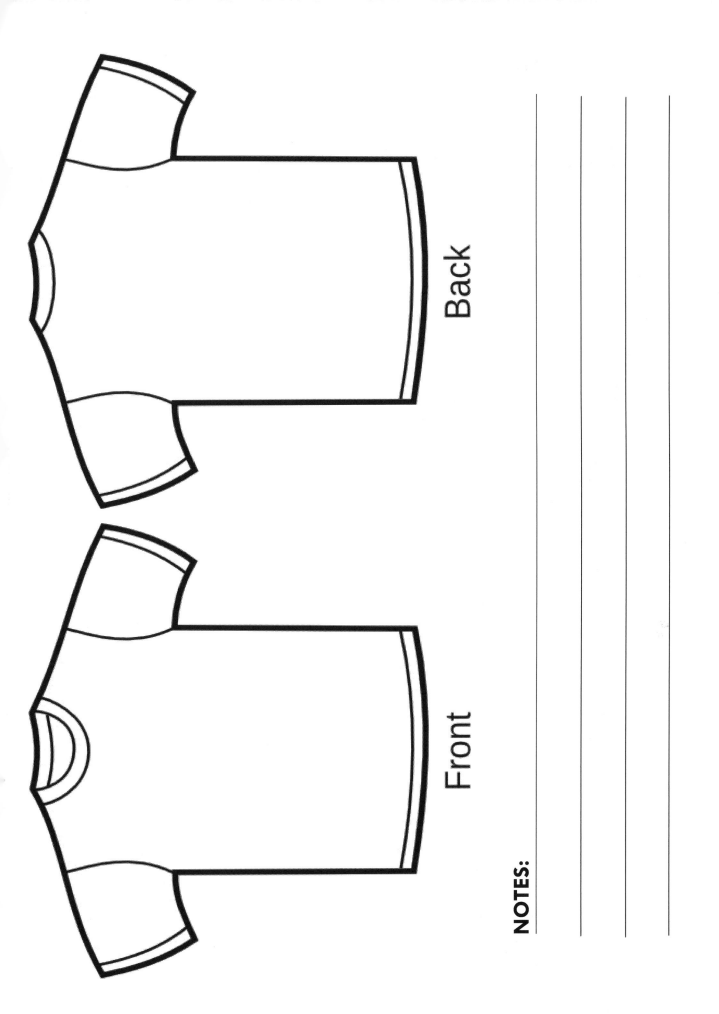

Back

Front

NOTES:

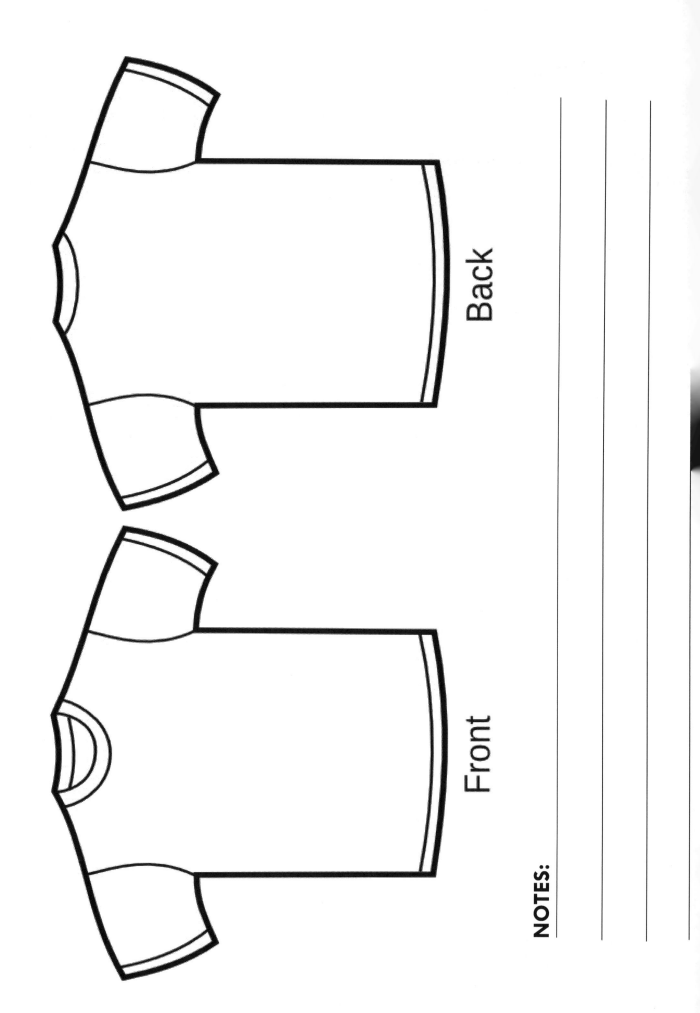

Back

Front

NOTES:

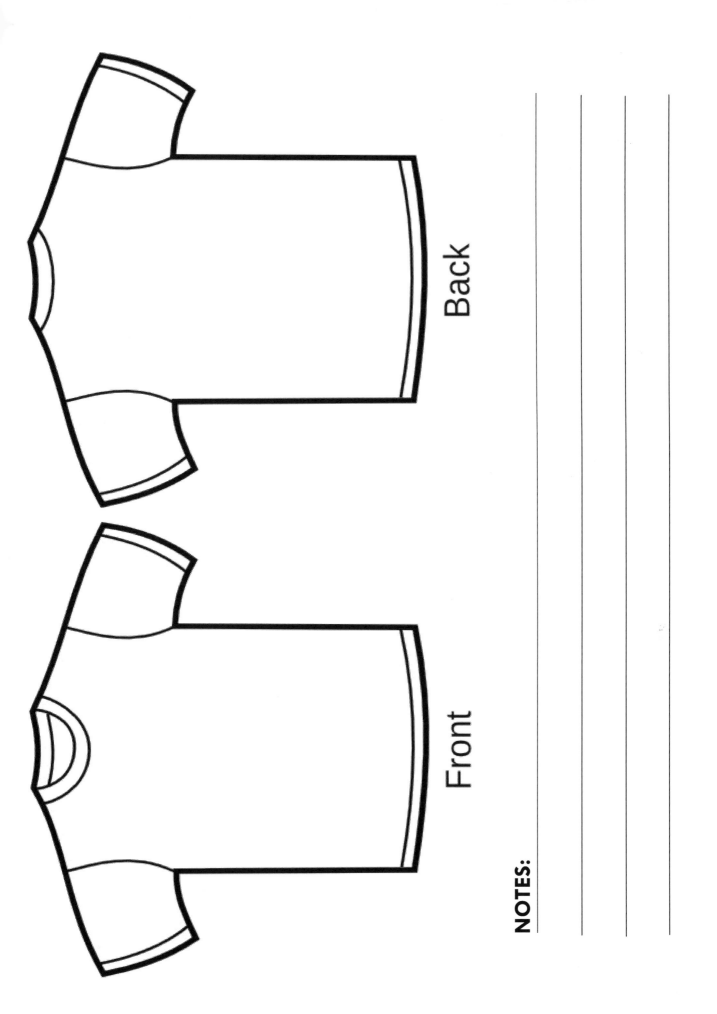

Back

Front

NOTES:

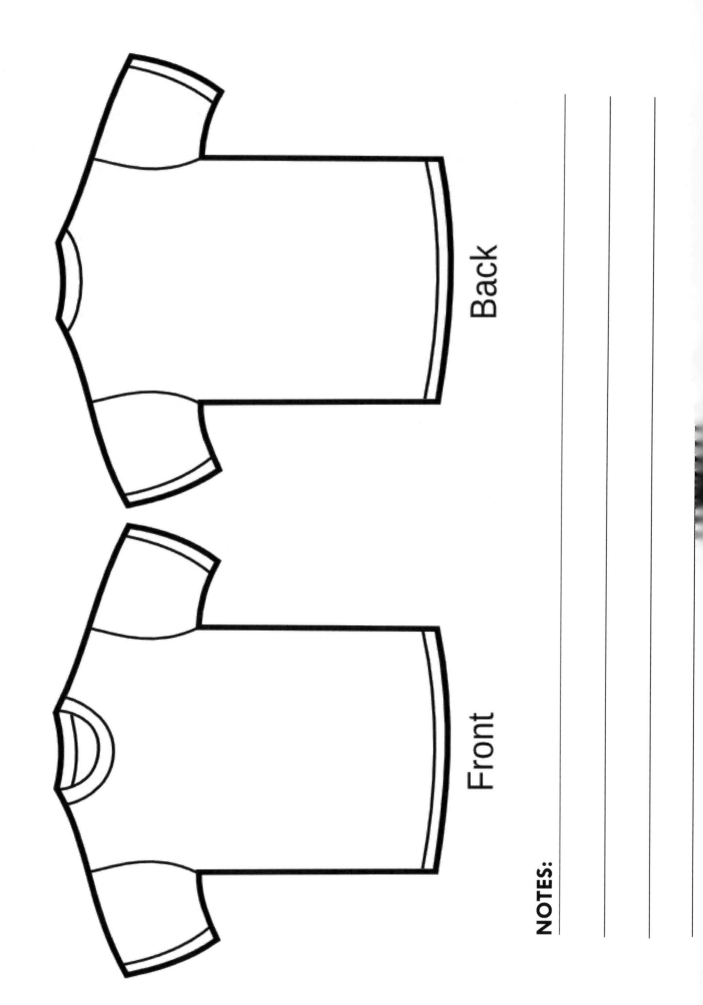

Back

Front

NOTES:

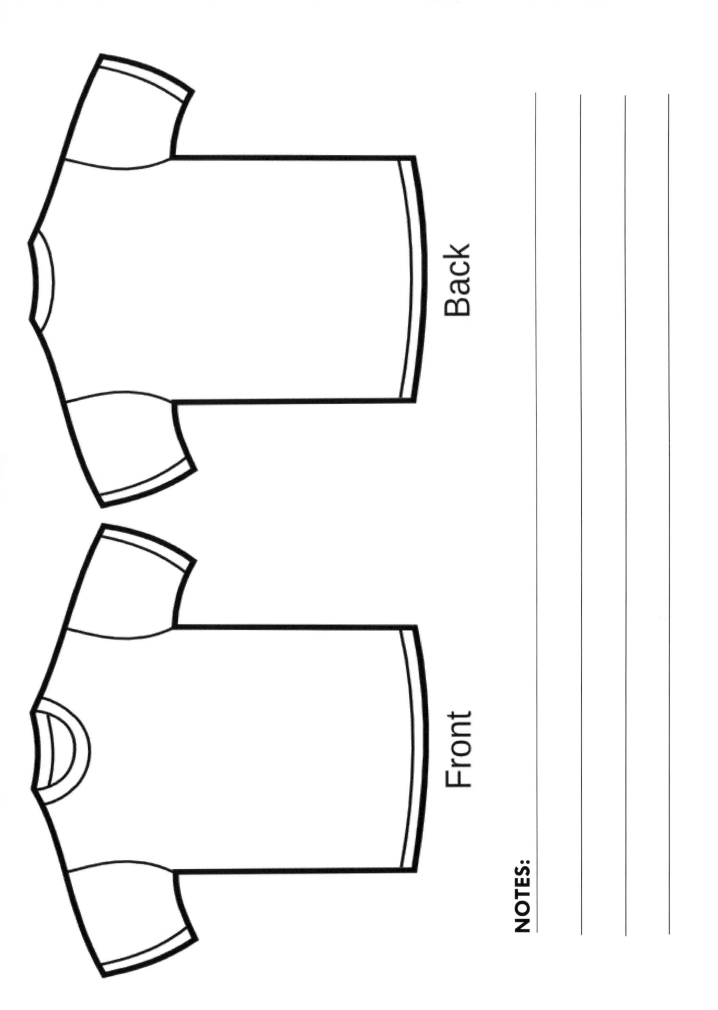

Back

Front

NOTES:

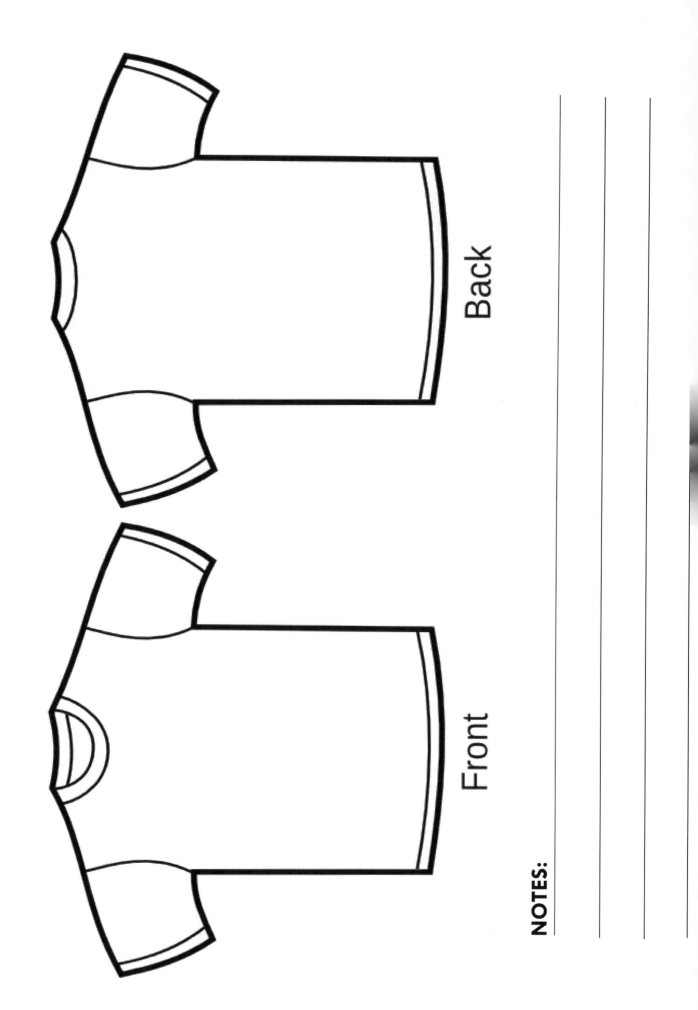

Back

Front

NOTES:

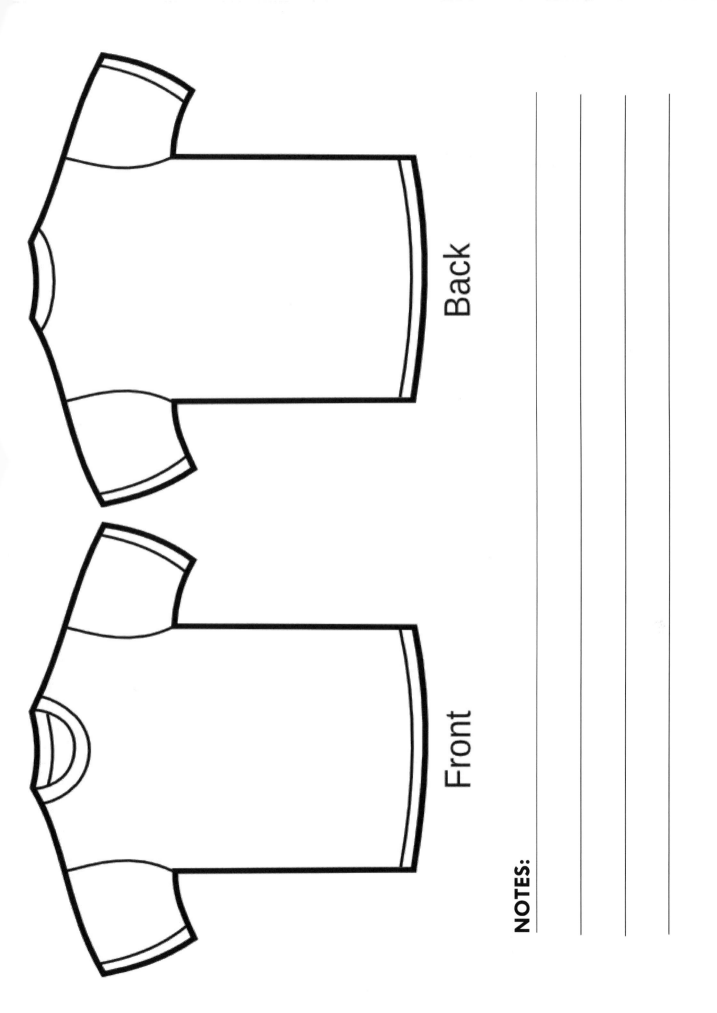

Back

Front

NOTES:

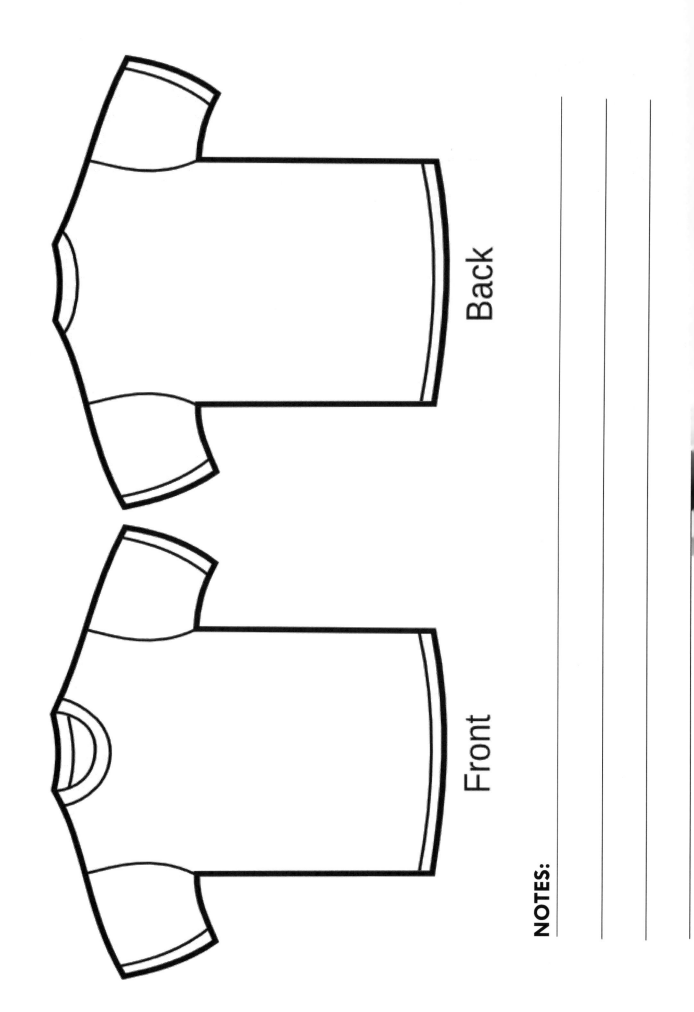

Back

Front

NOTES:

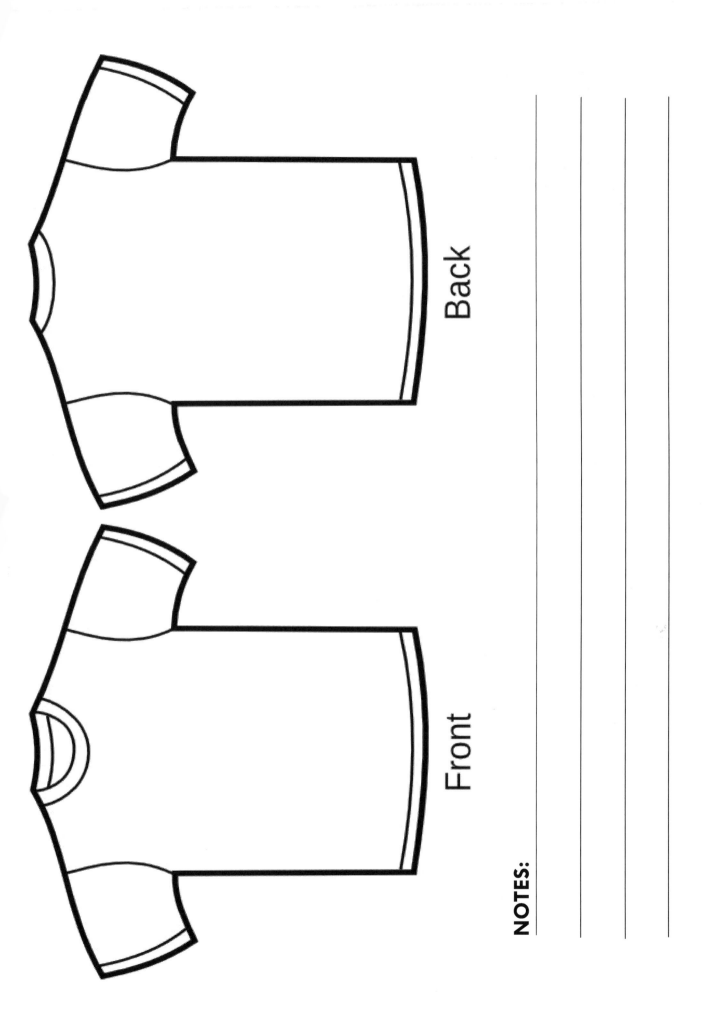

Back

Front

NOTES:

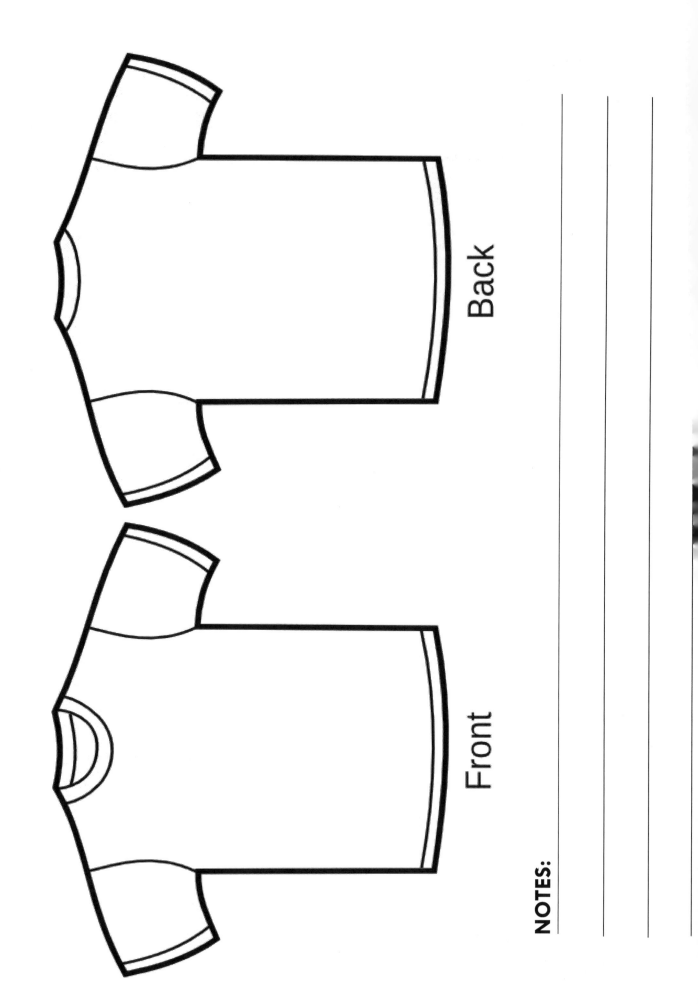

Back

Front

NOTES:

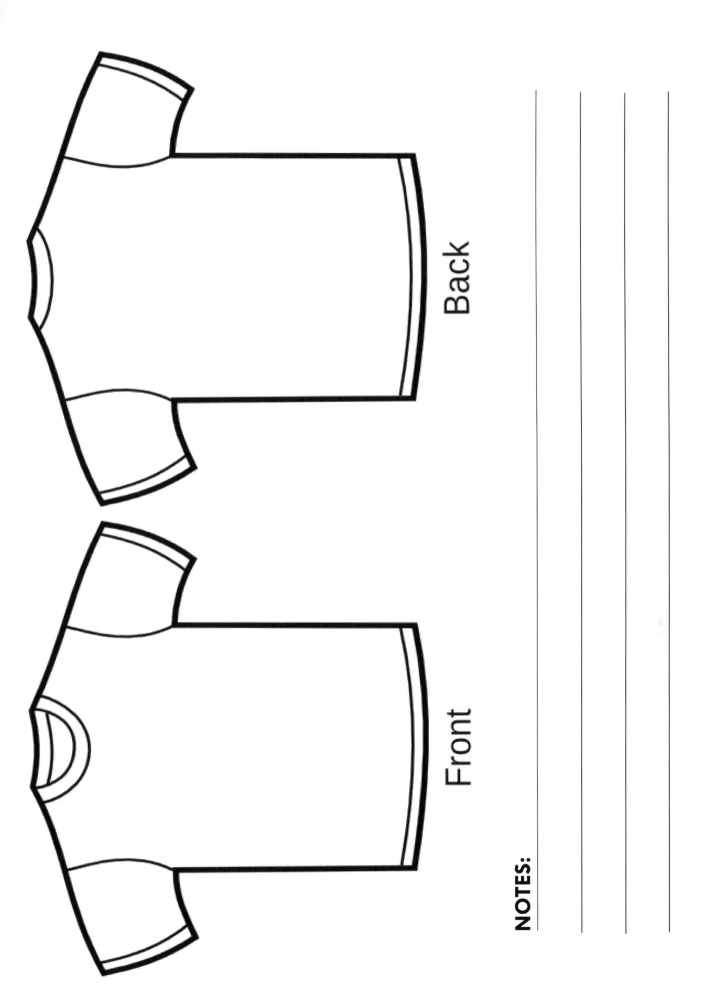

Back

Front

NOTES:

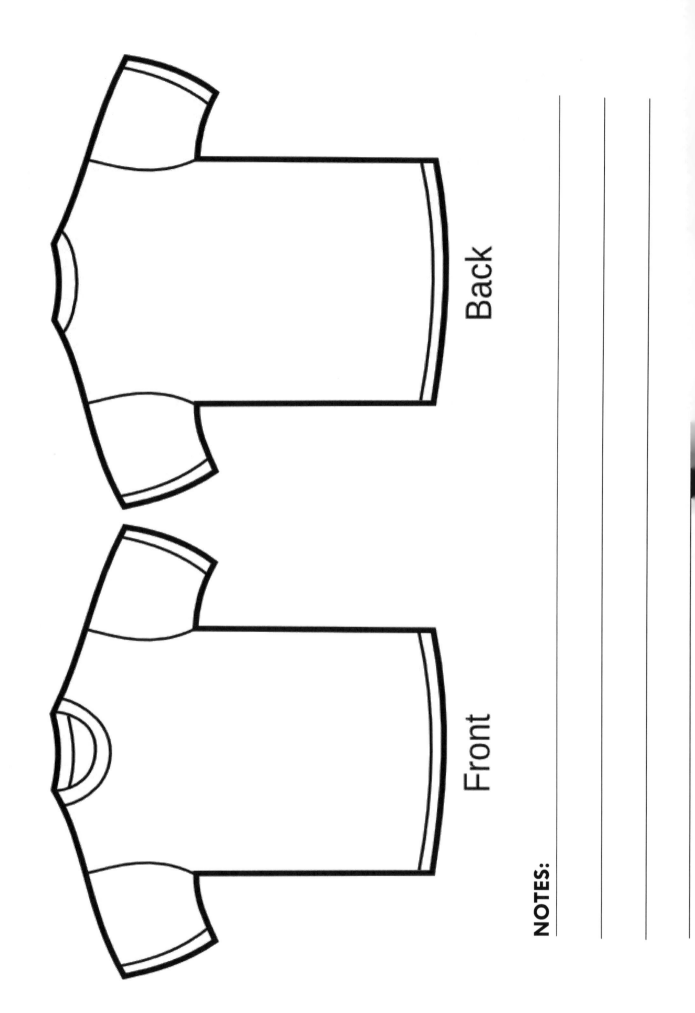

Back

Front

NOTES:

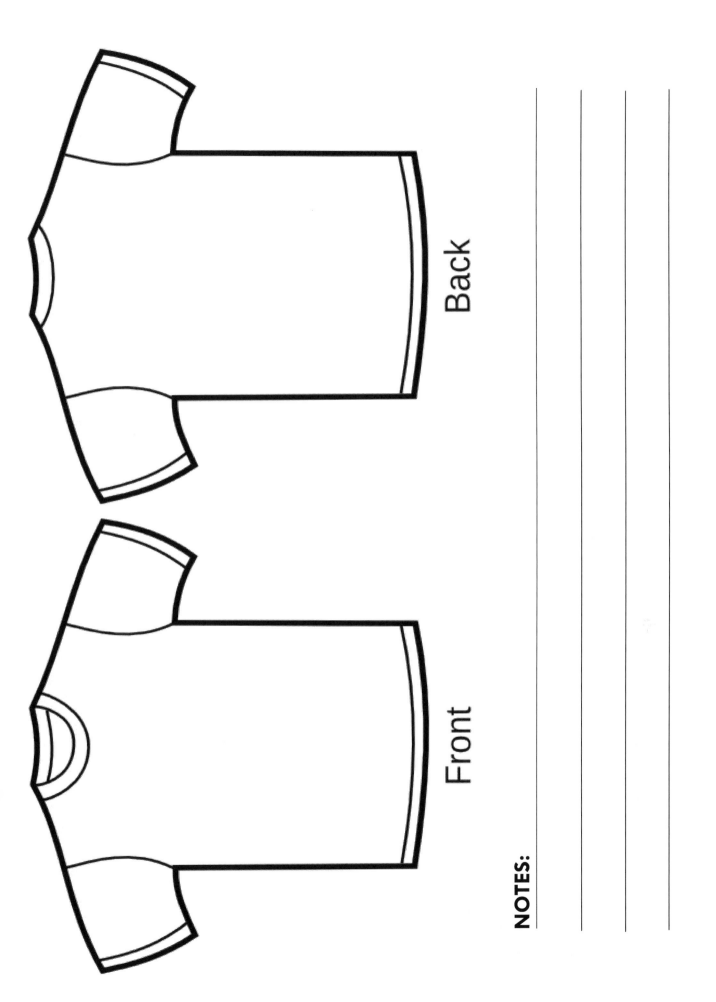

Back

Front

NOTES:

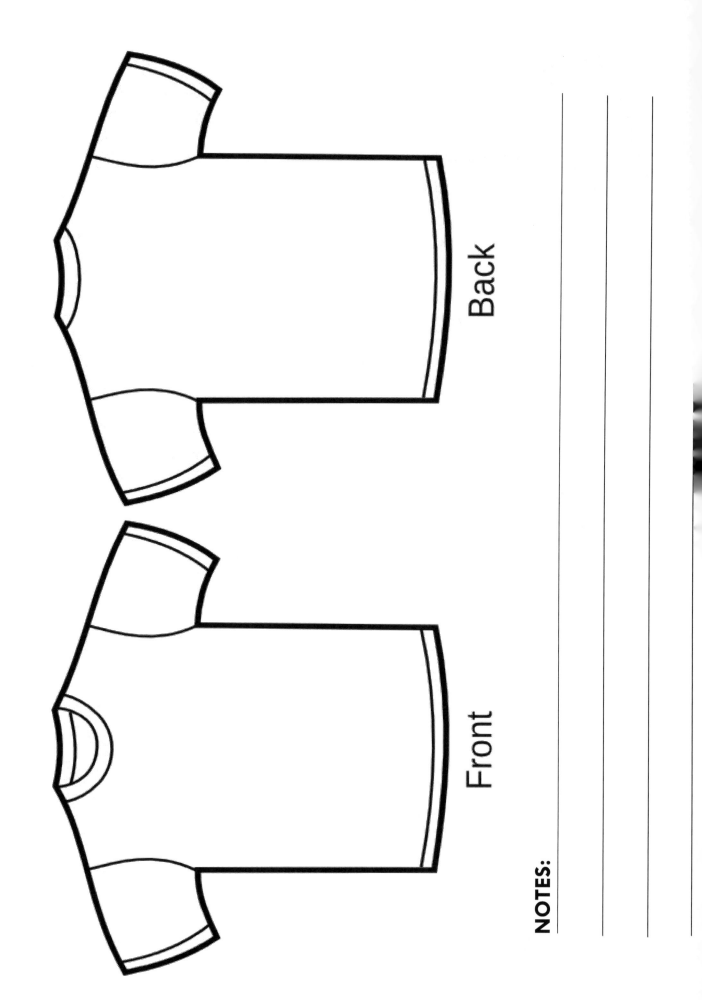

Back

Front

NOTES:

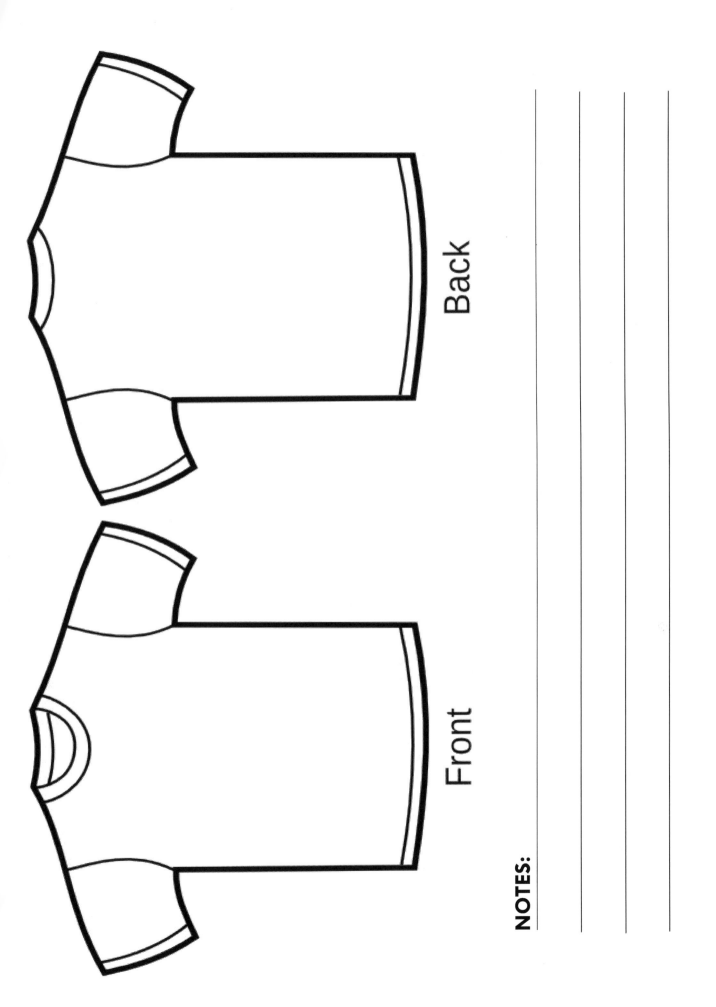

Back

Front

NOTES:

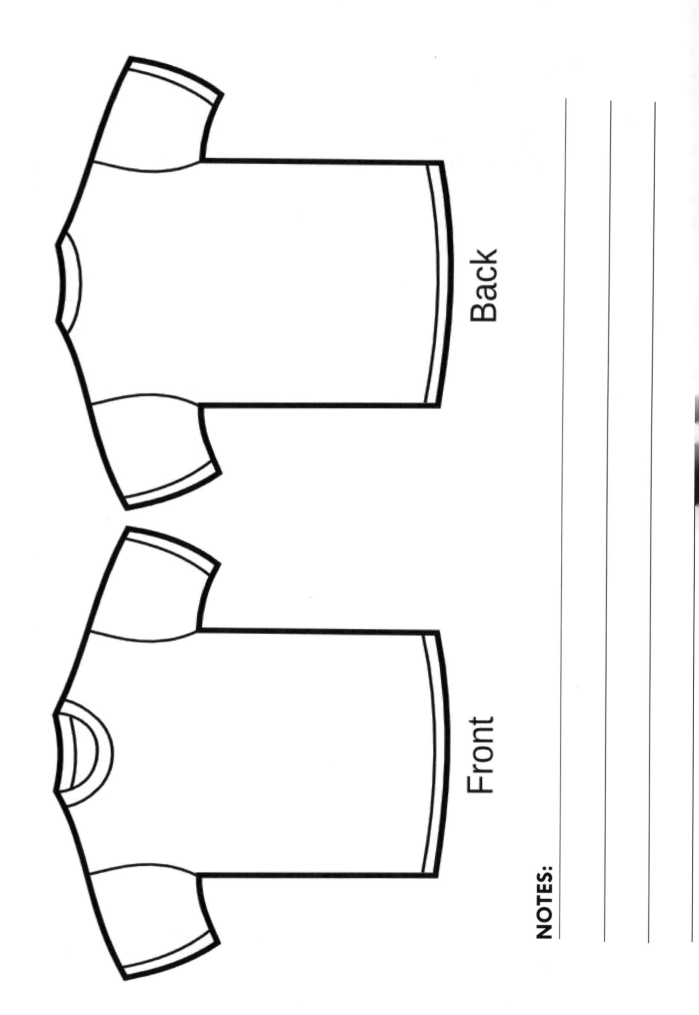

Back

Front

NOTES:

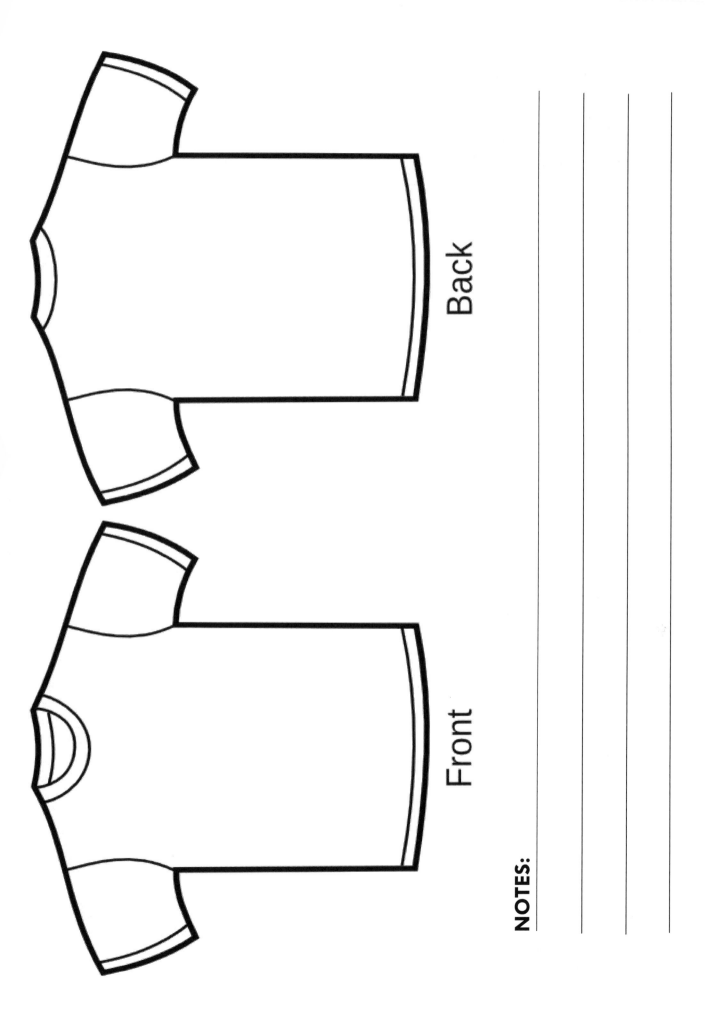

Back

Front

NOTES:

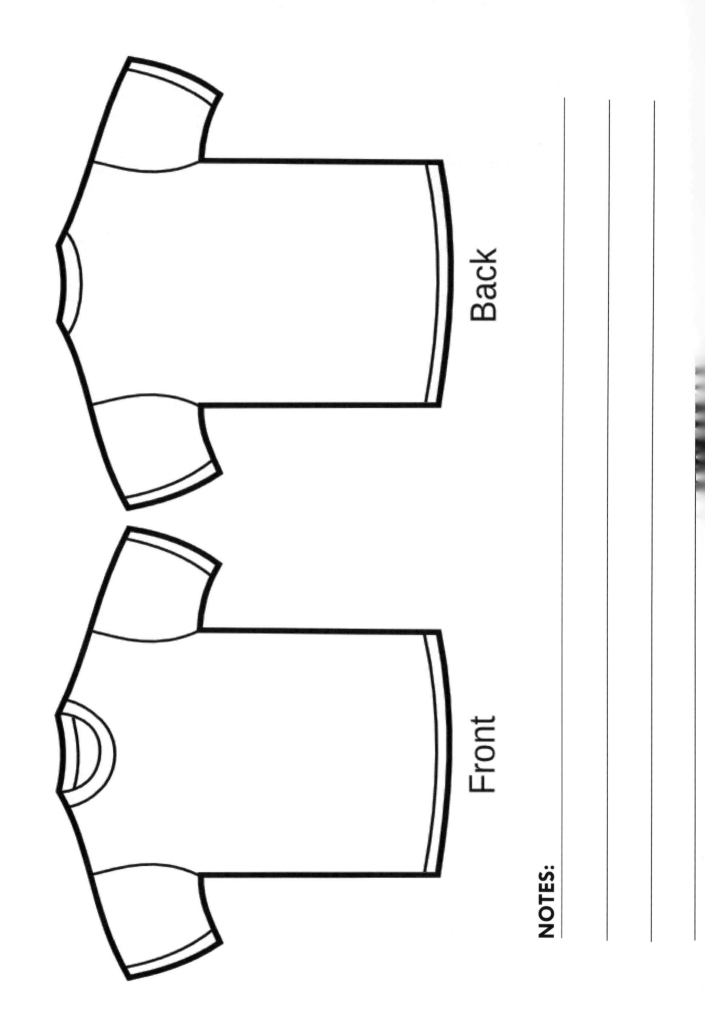

Back

Front

NOTES:

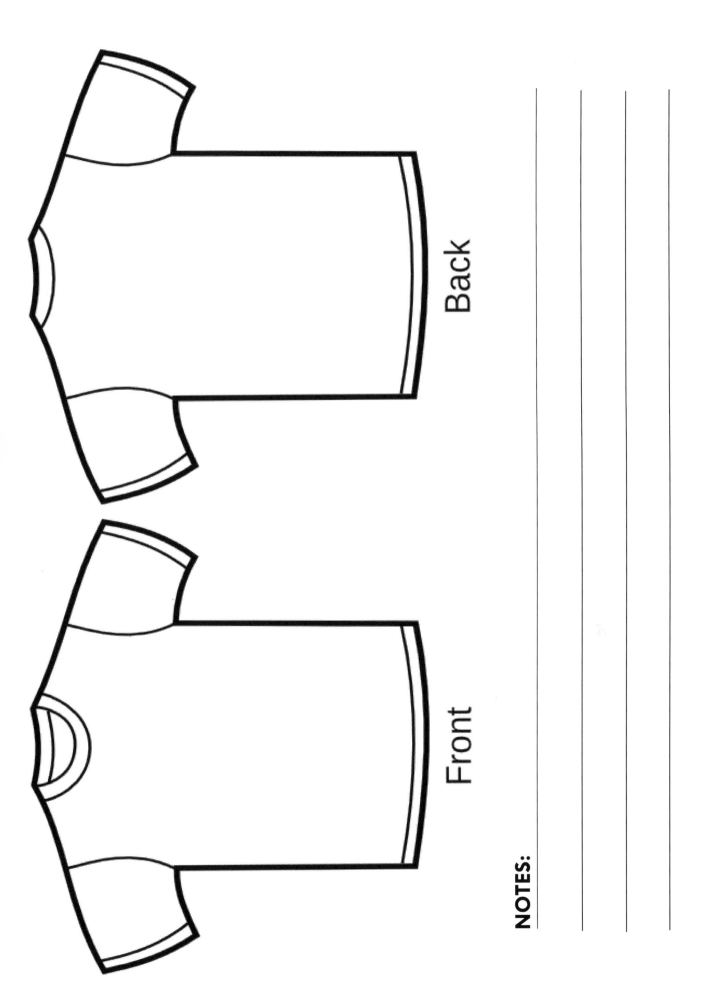

Back

Front

NOTES:

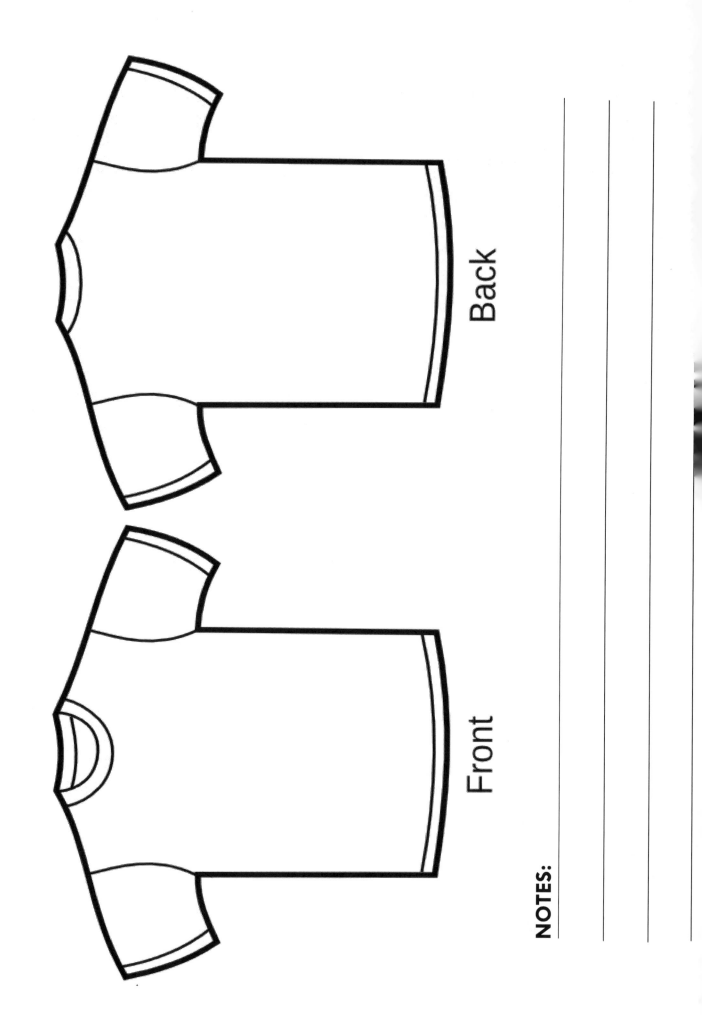

Back

Front

NOTES:

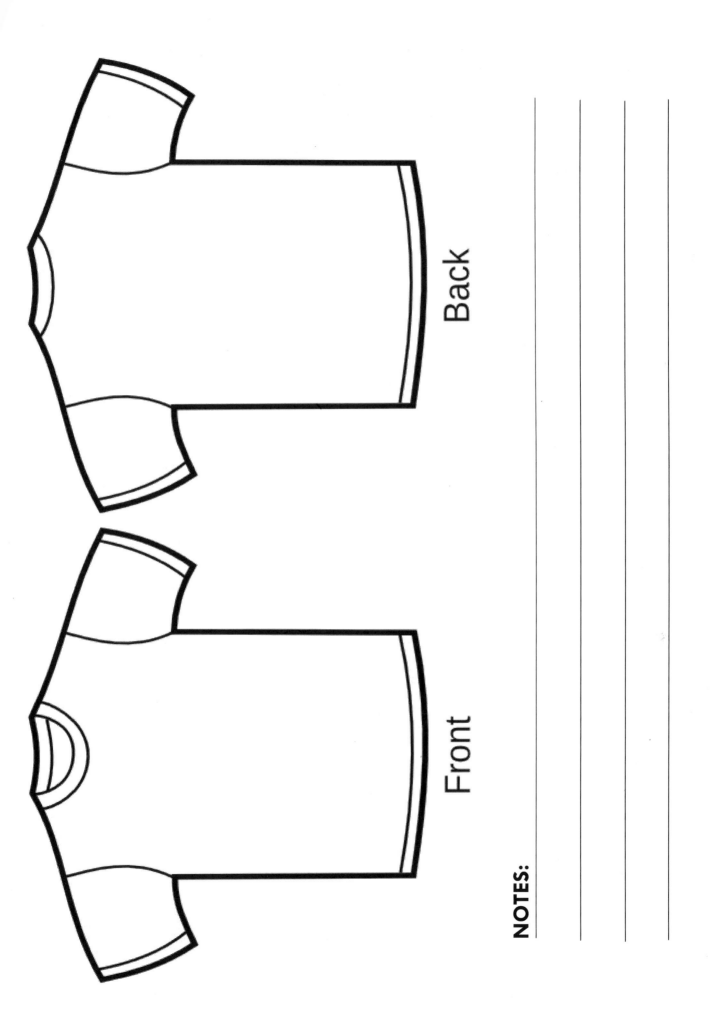

Back

Front

NOTES:

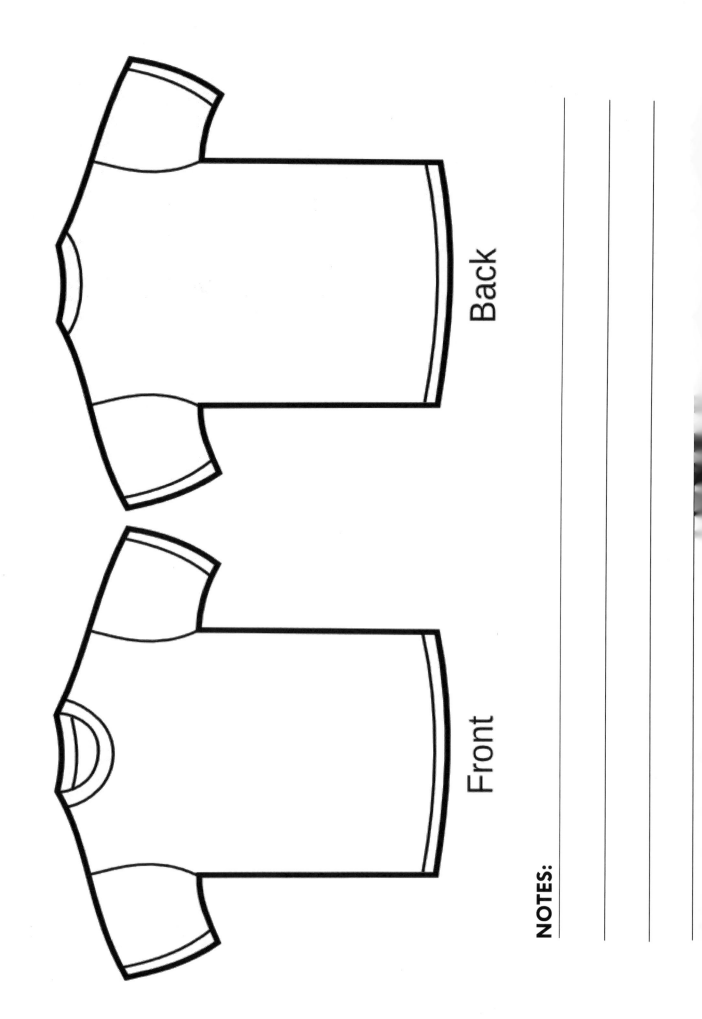

Back

Front

NOTES:

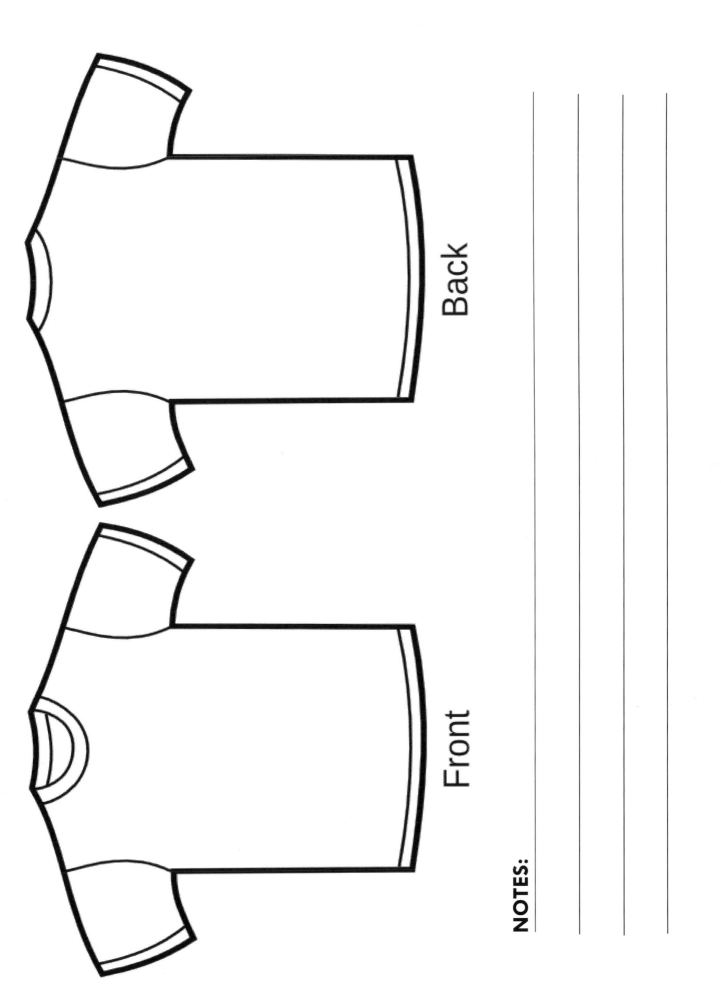

Back

Front

NOTES:

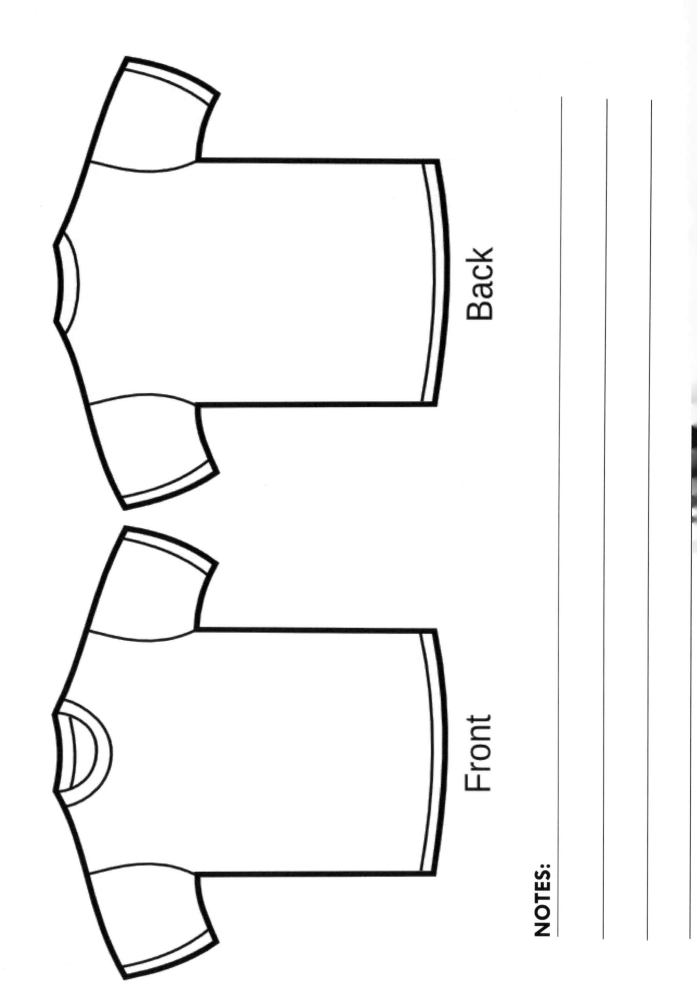

Back

Front

NOTES:

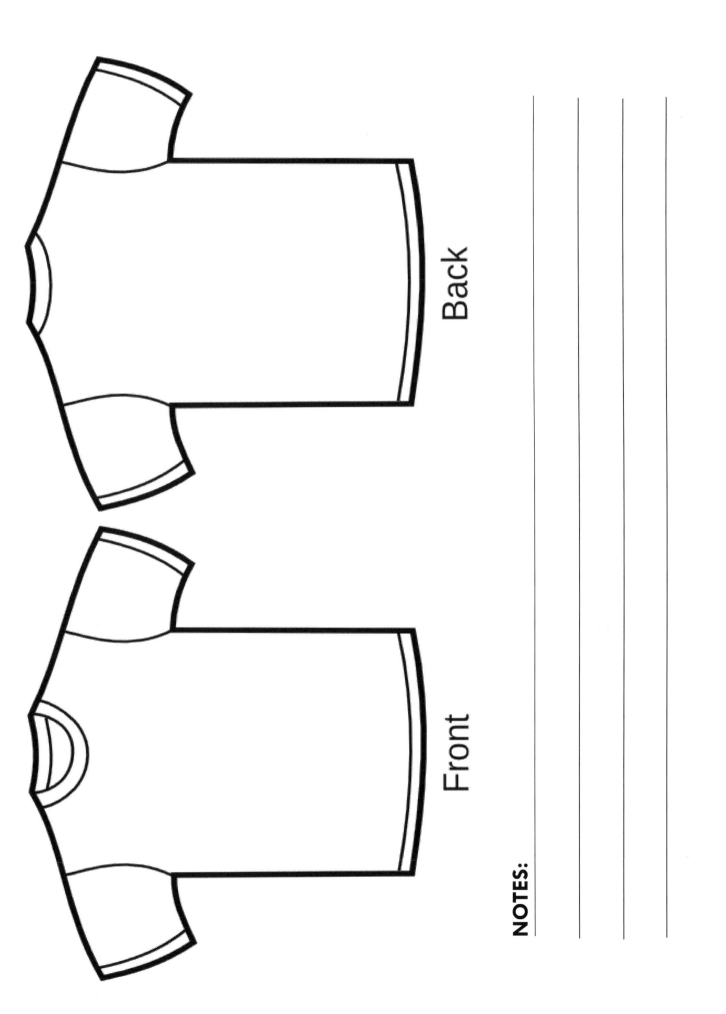

Back

Front

NOTES:

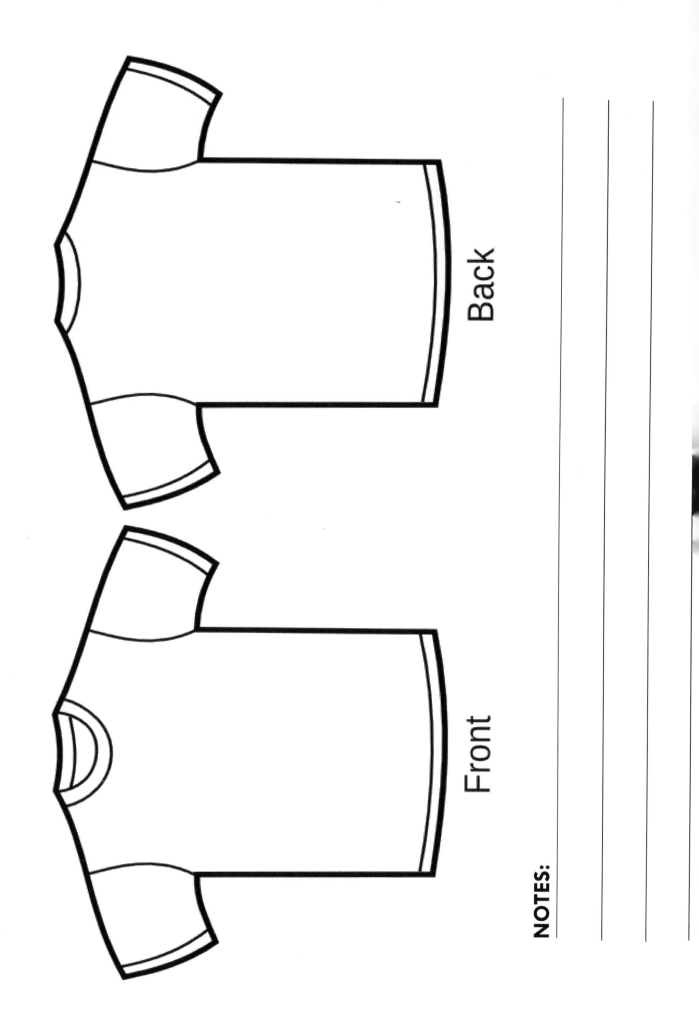

Back

Front

NOTES:

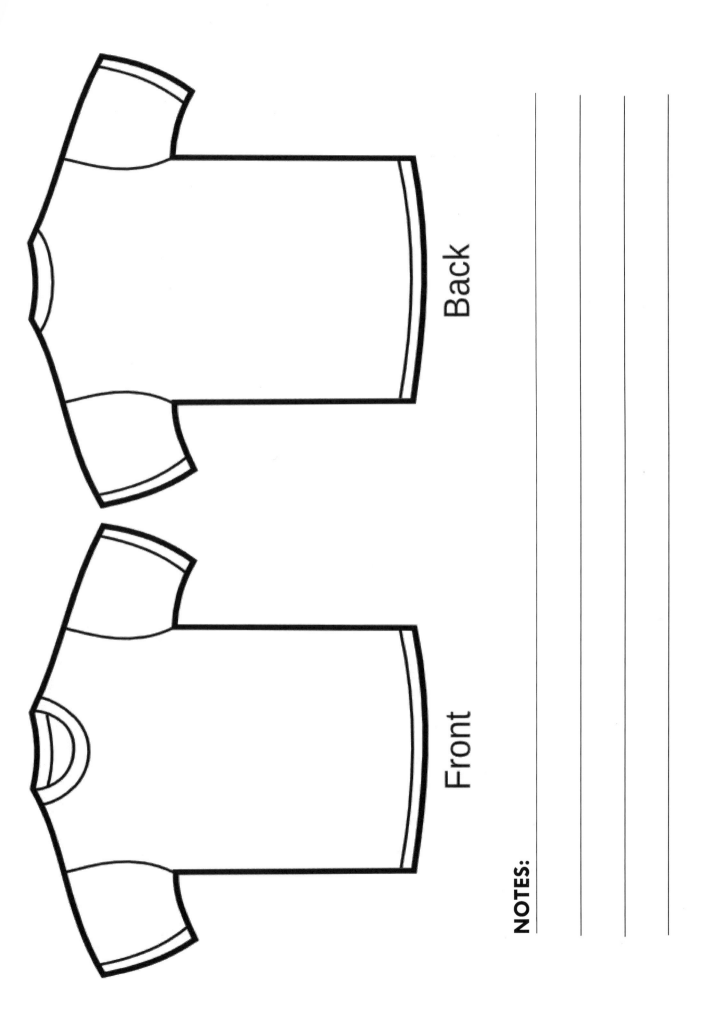

Back

Front

NOTES:

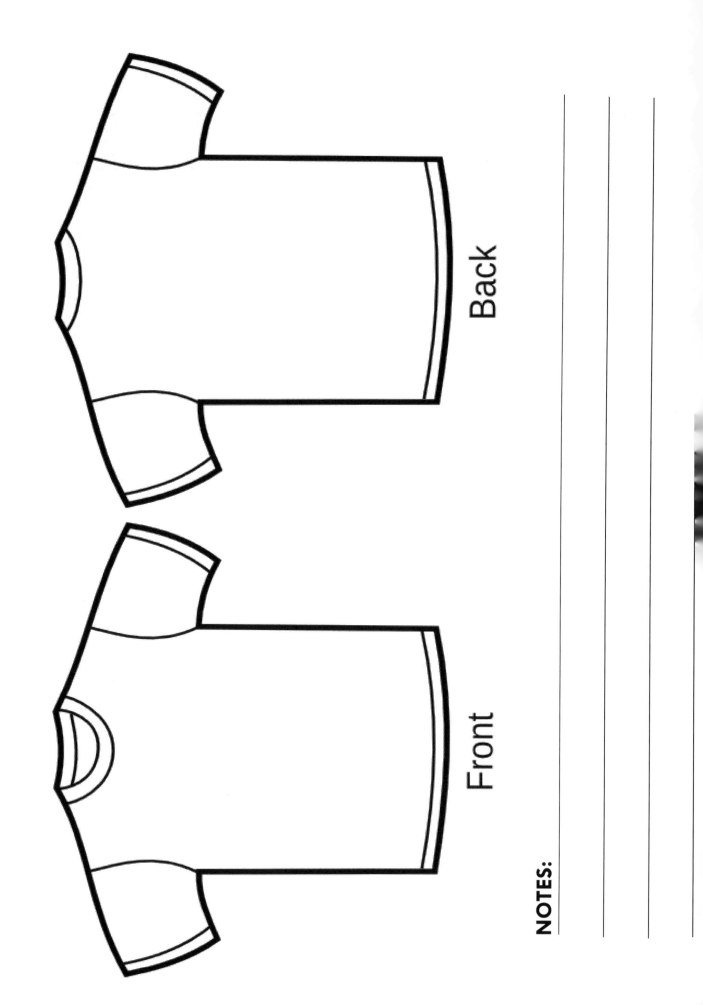

Back

Front

NOTES:

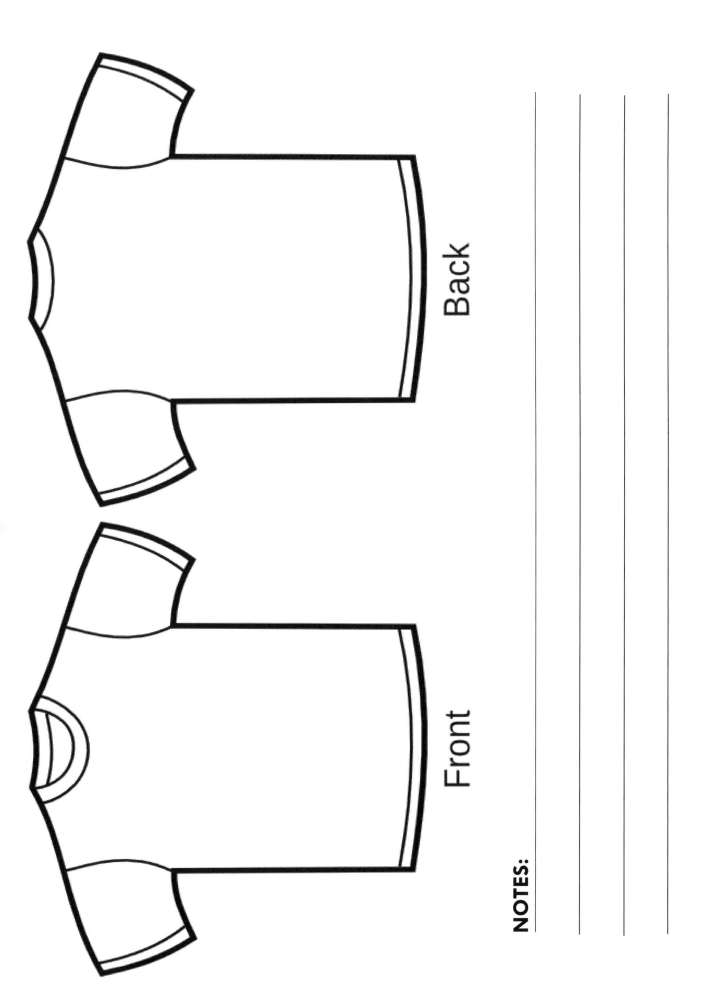

Back

Front

NOTES:

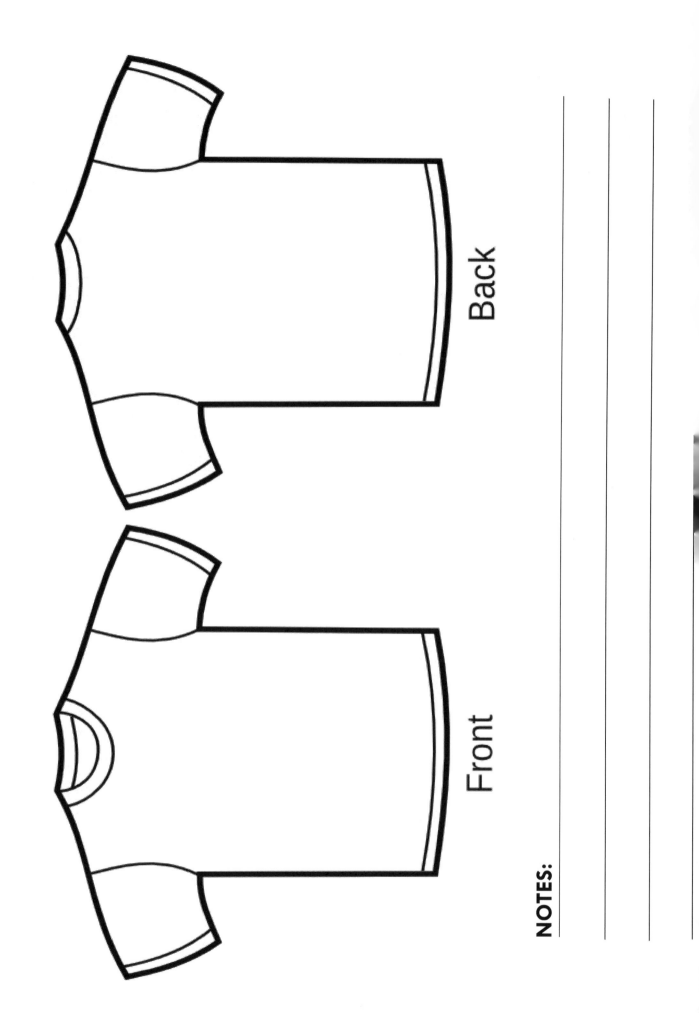

Back

Front

NOTES:

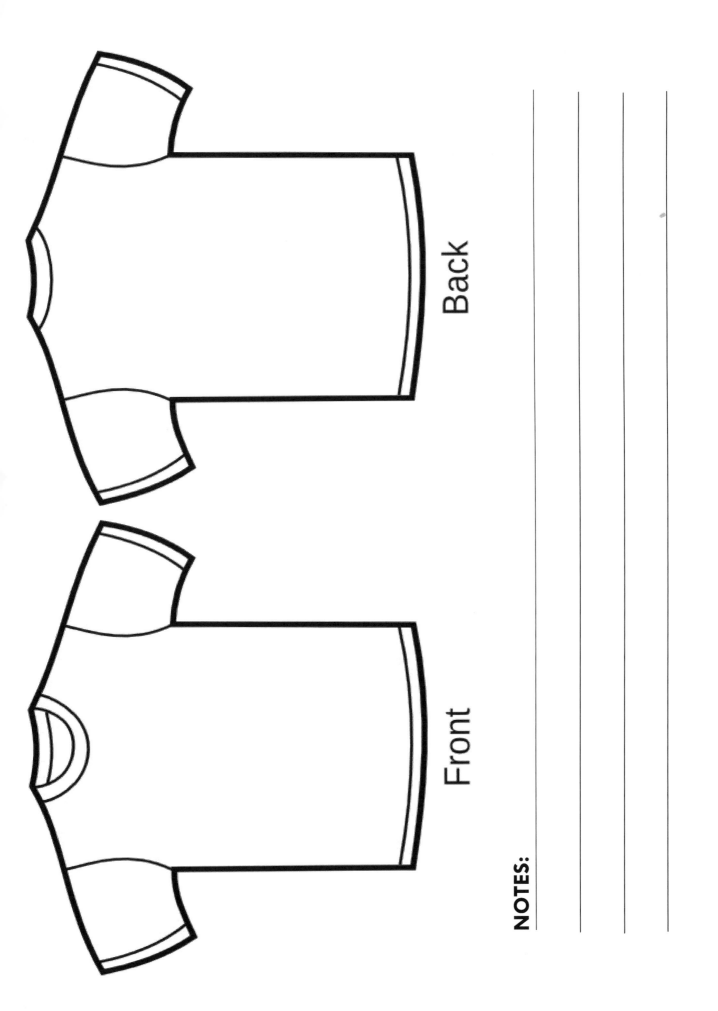

Back

Front

NOTES:

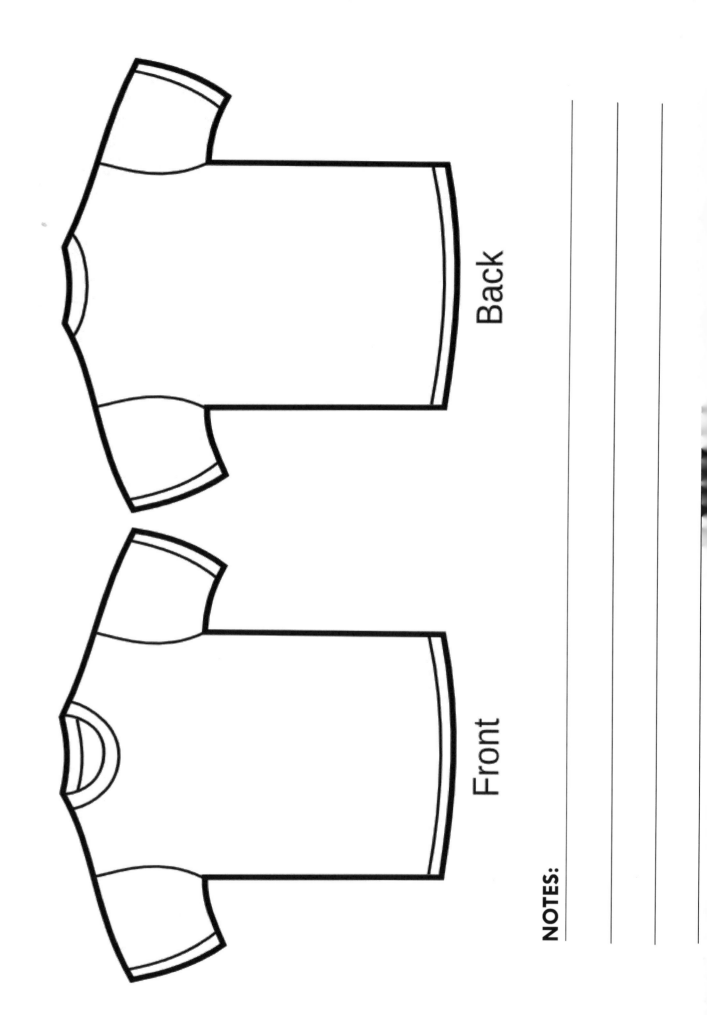

Back

Front

NOTES:

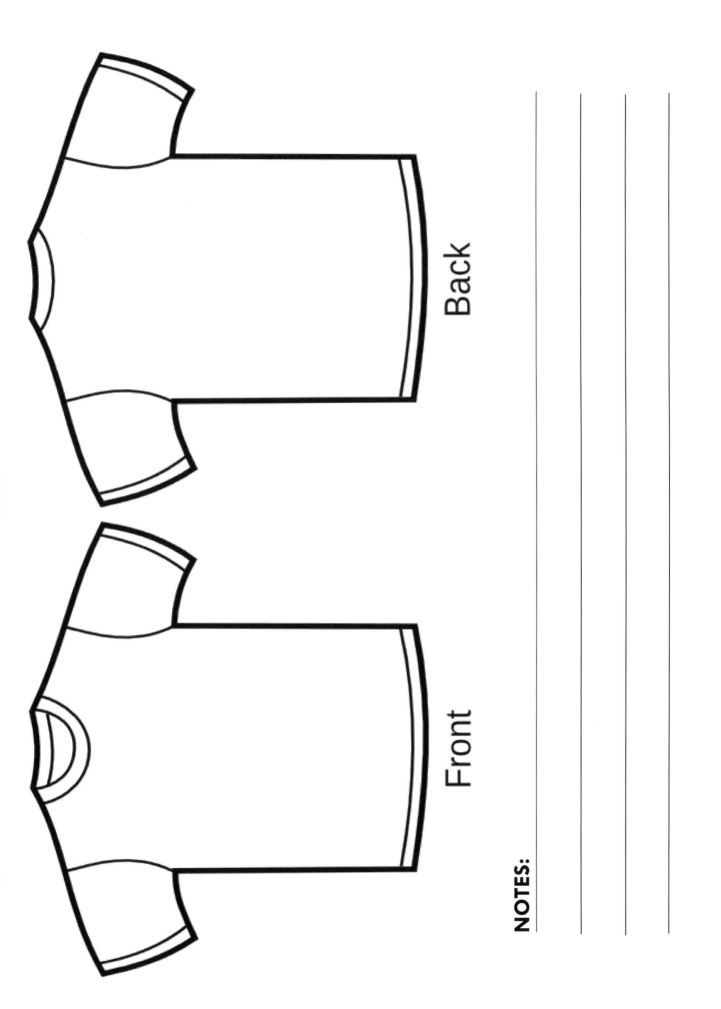

Back

Front

NOTES:

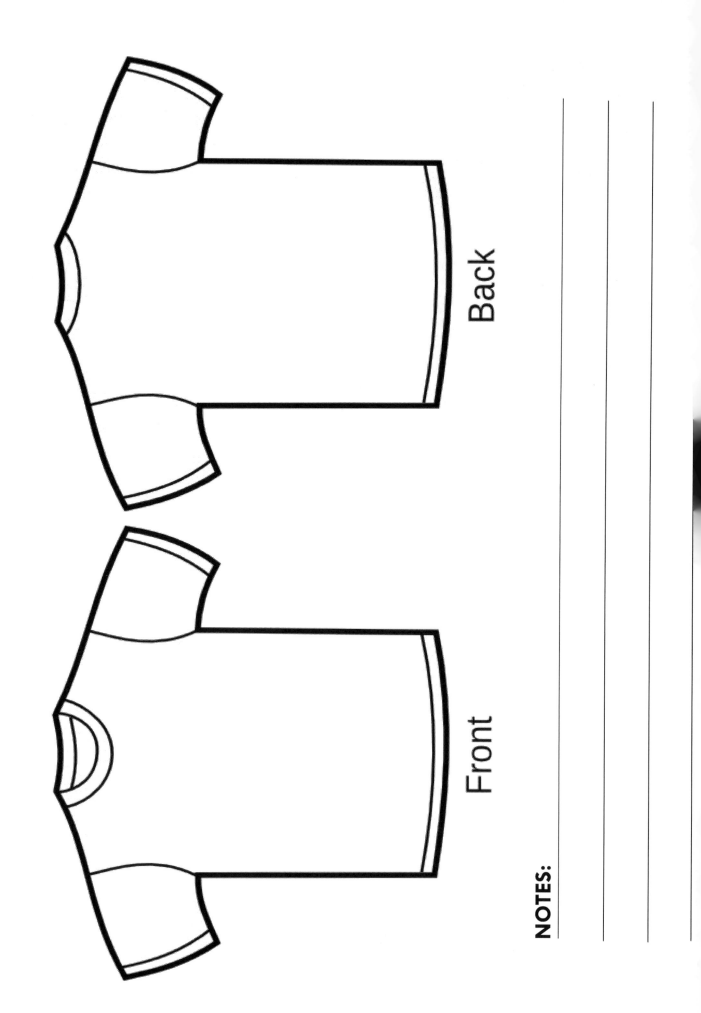

Back

Front

NOTES:

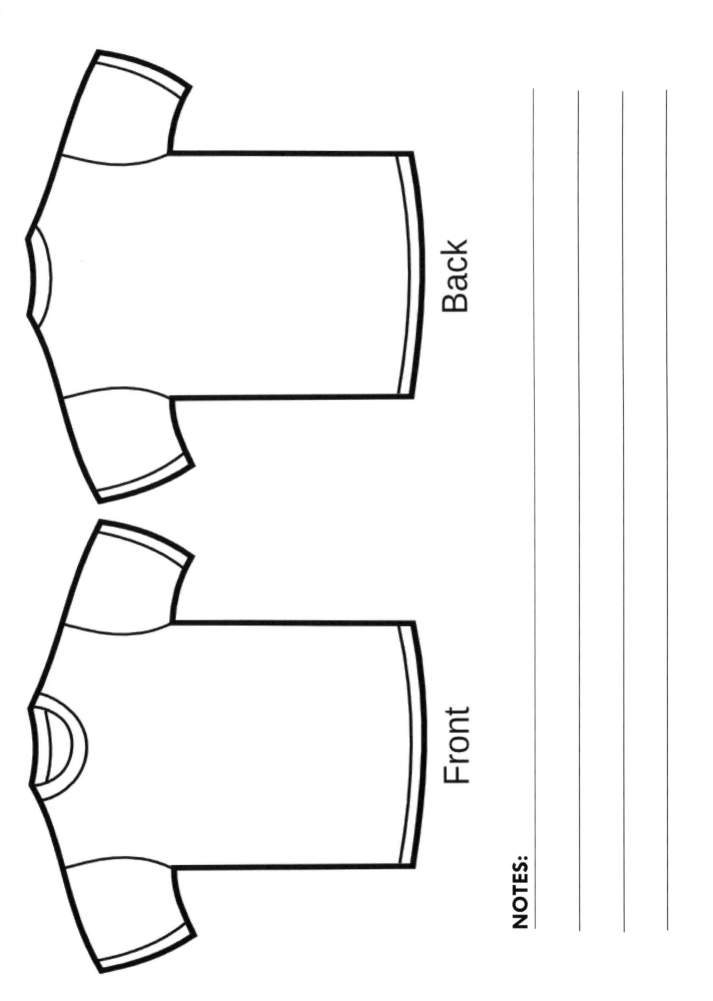

Back

Front

NOTES:

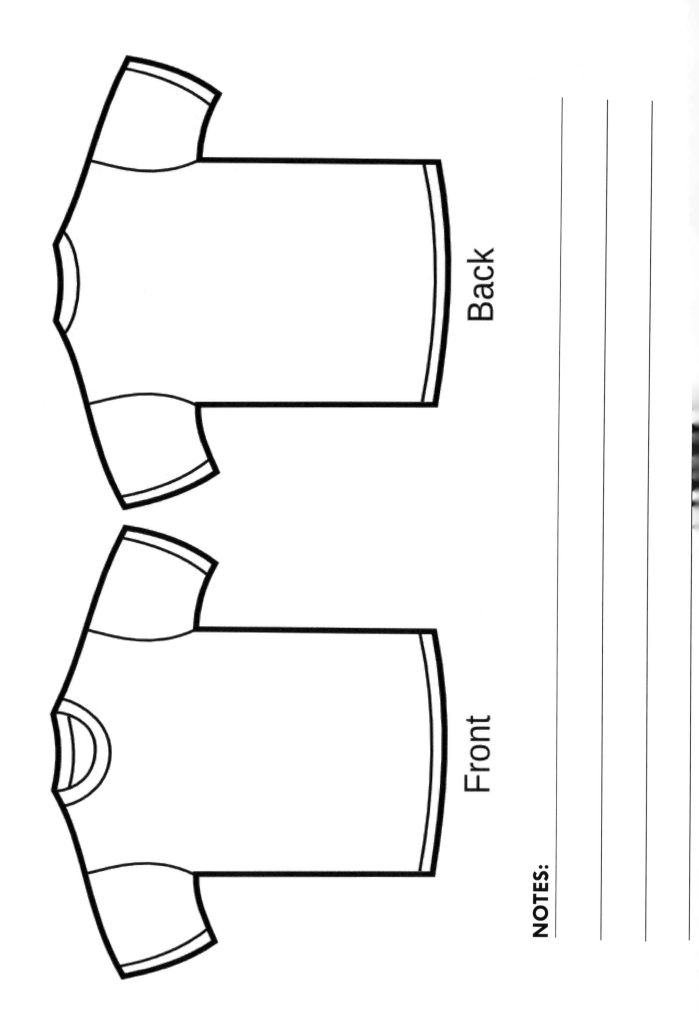

Back

Front

NOTES:

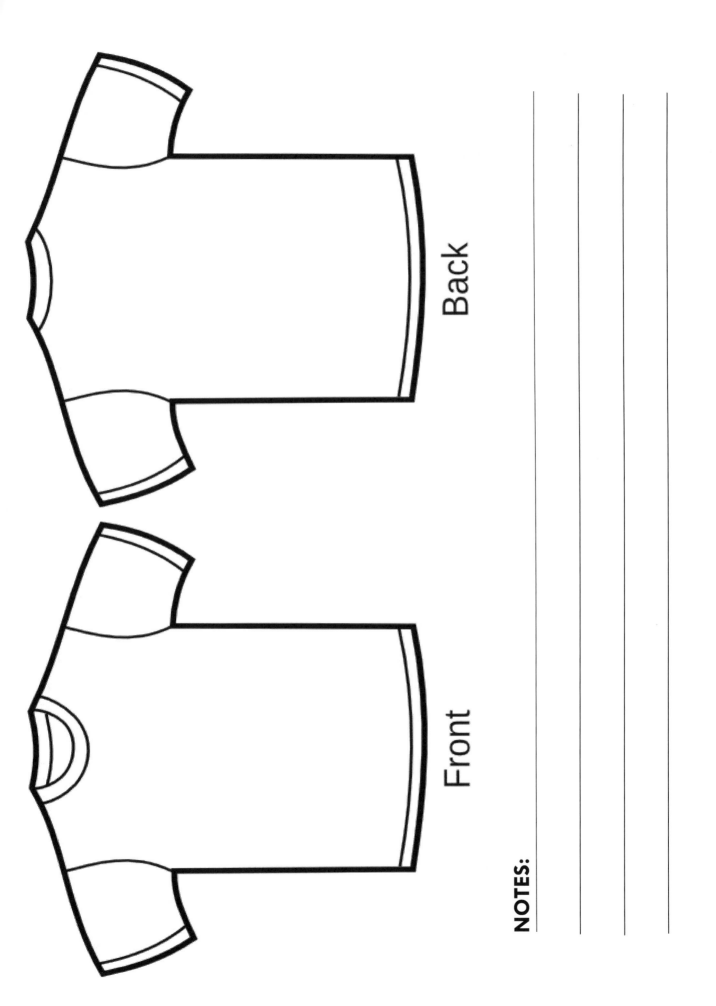

Back

Front

NOTES:

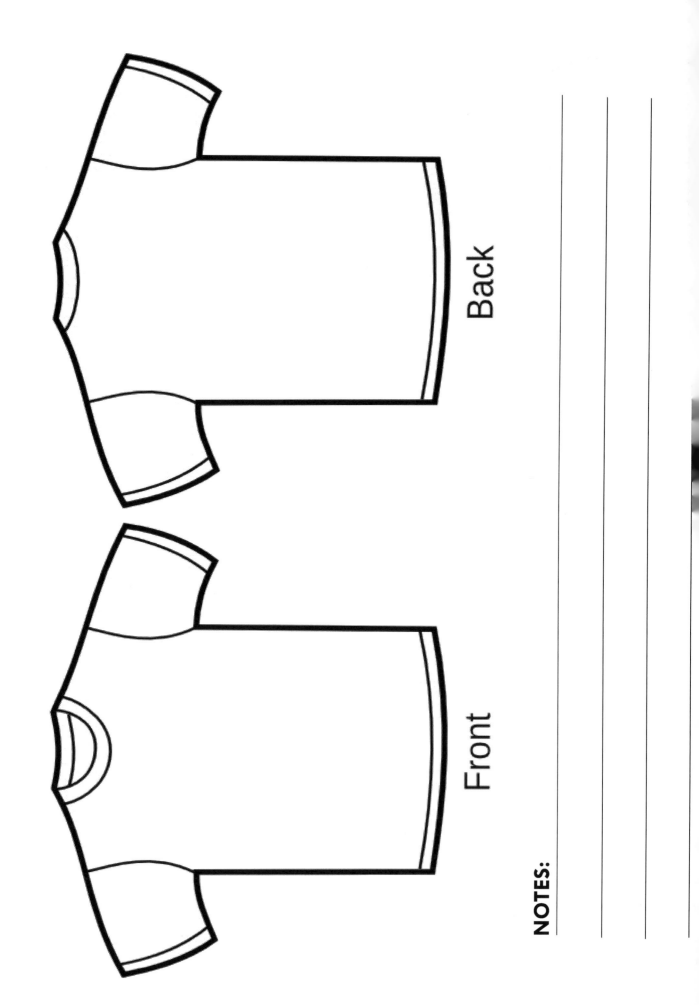

Back

Front

NOTES:

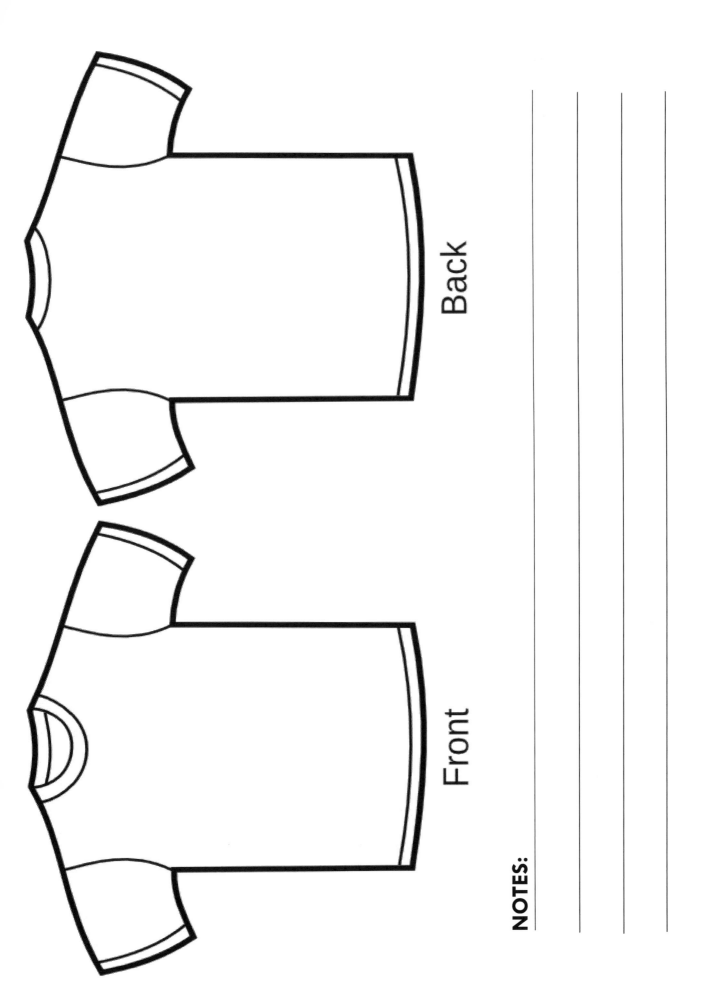

Back

Front

NOTES:

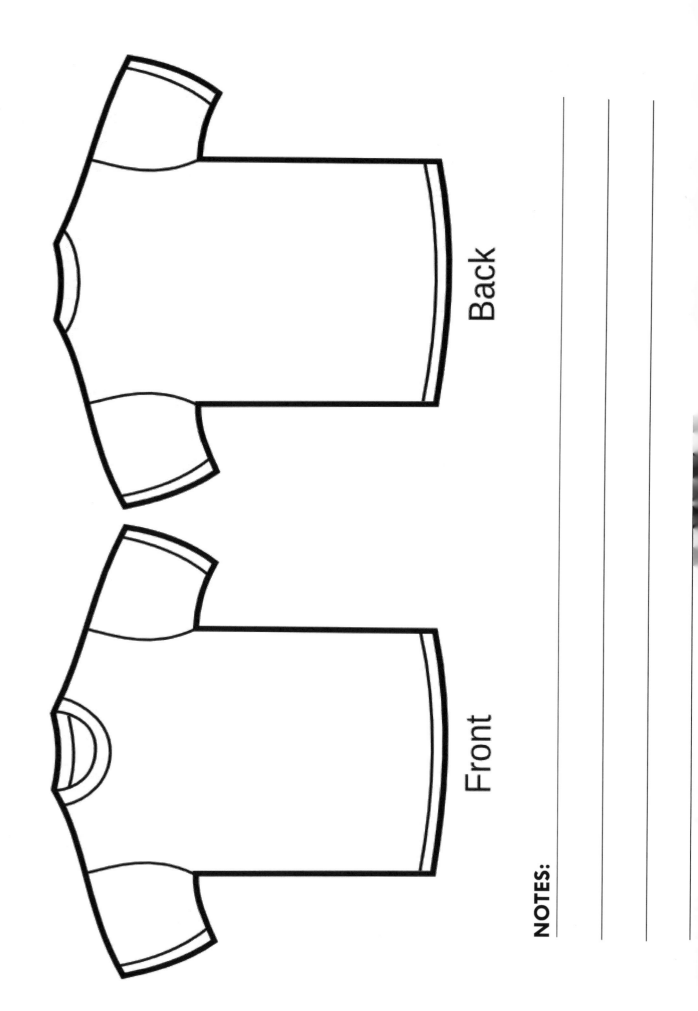

Back

Front

NOTES:

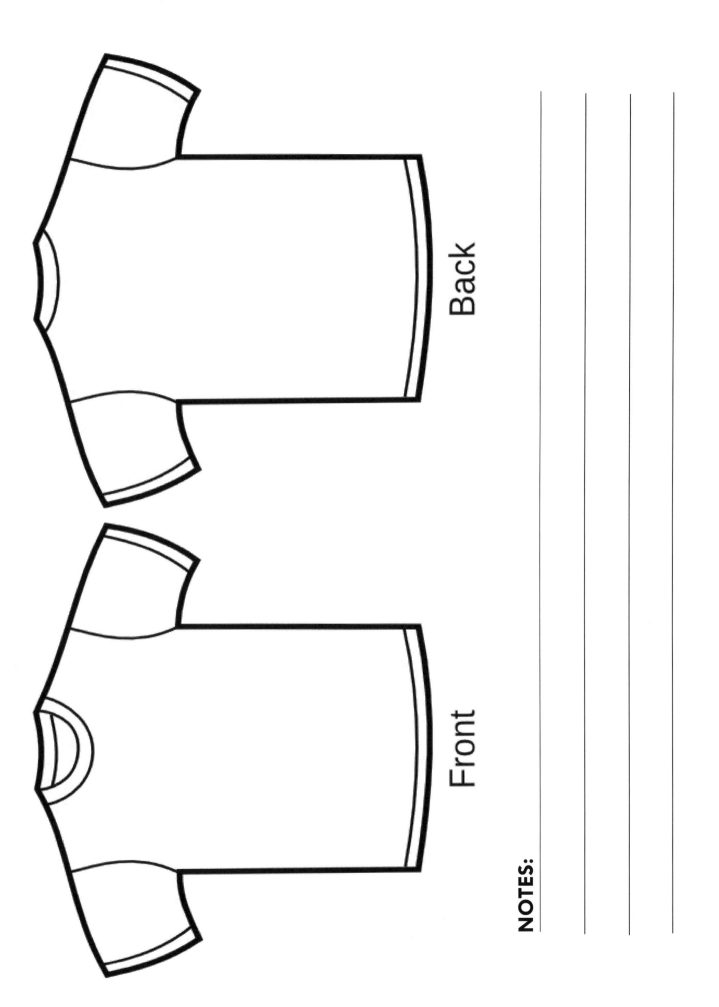

Back

Front

NOTES:

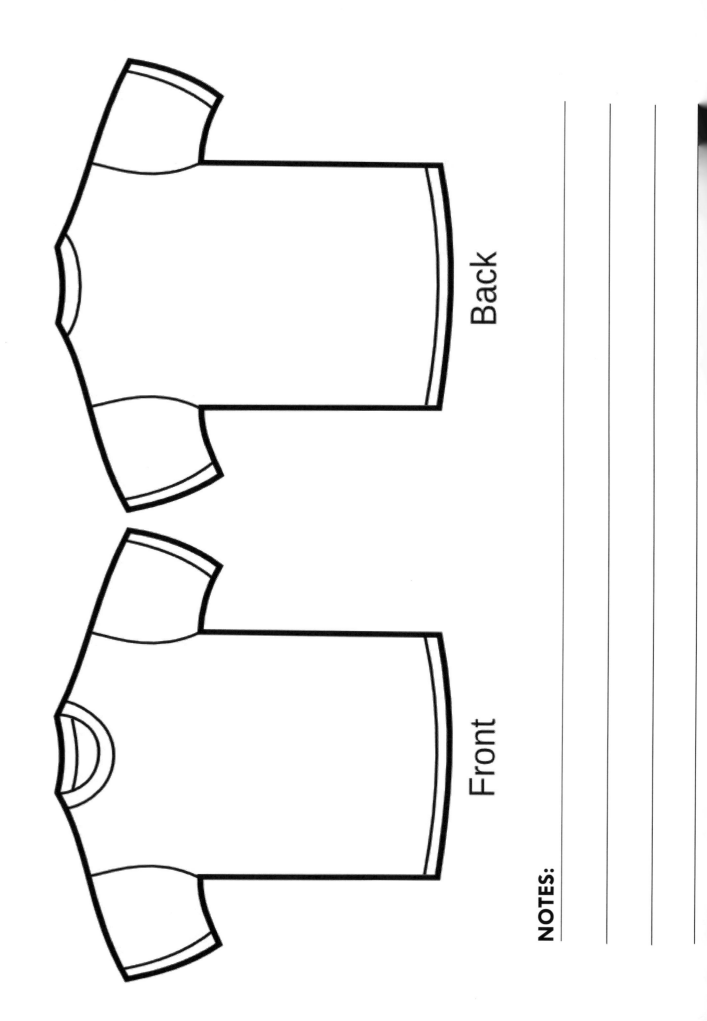

Back

Front

NOTES:

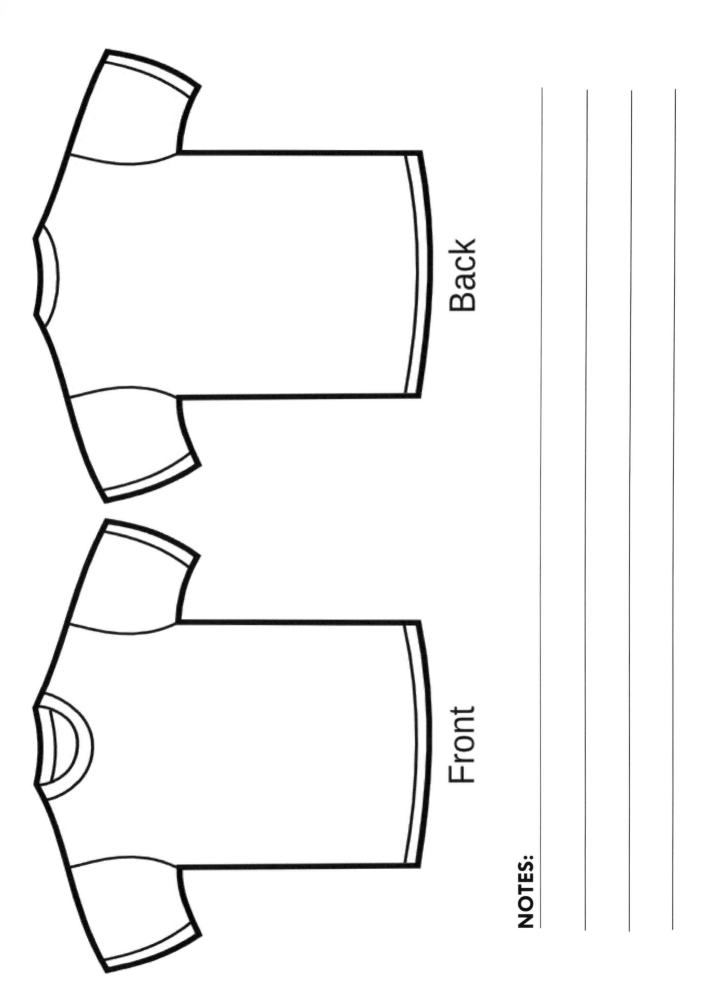

Back

Front

NOTES:

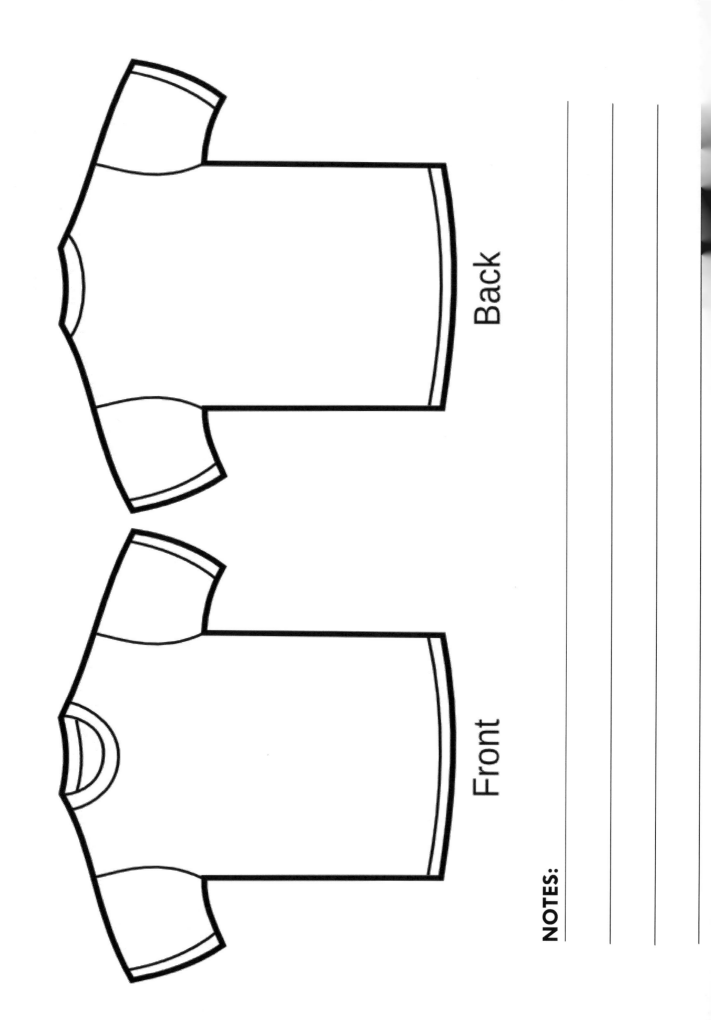

Back

Front

NOTES:

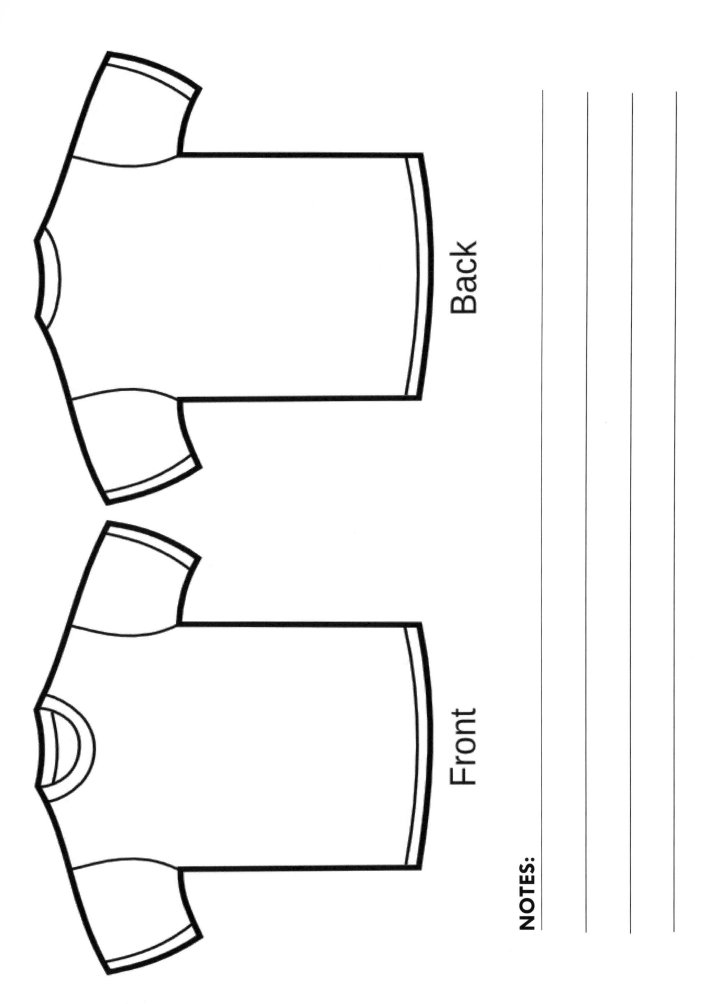

Back

Front

NOTES:

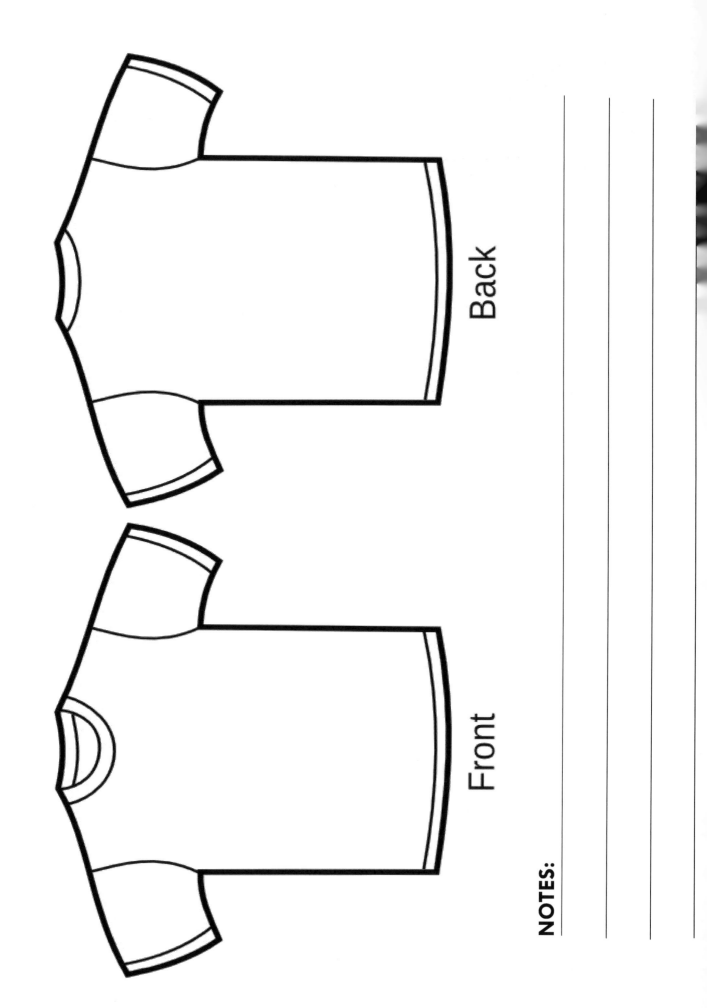

Back

Front

NOTES:

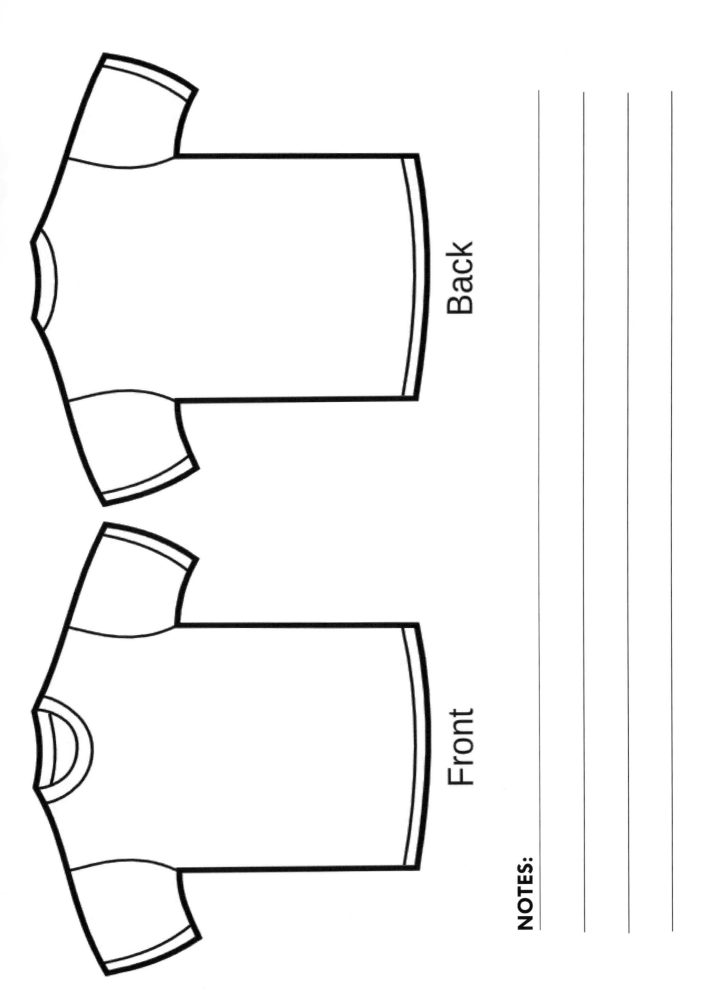

Back

Front

NOTES:

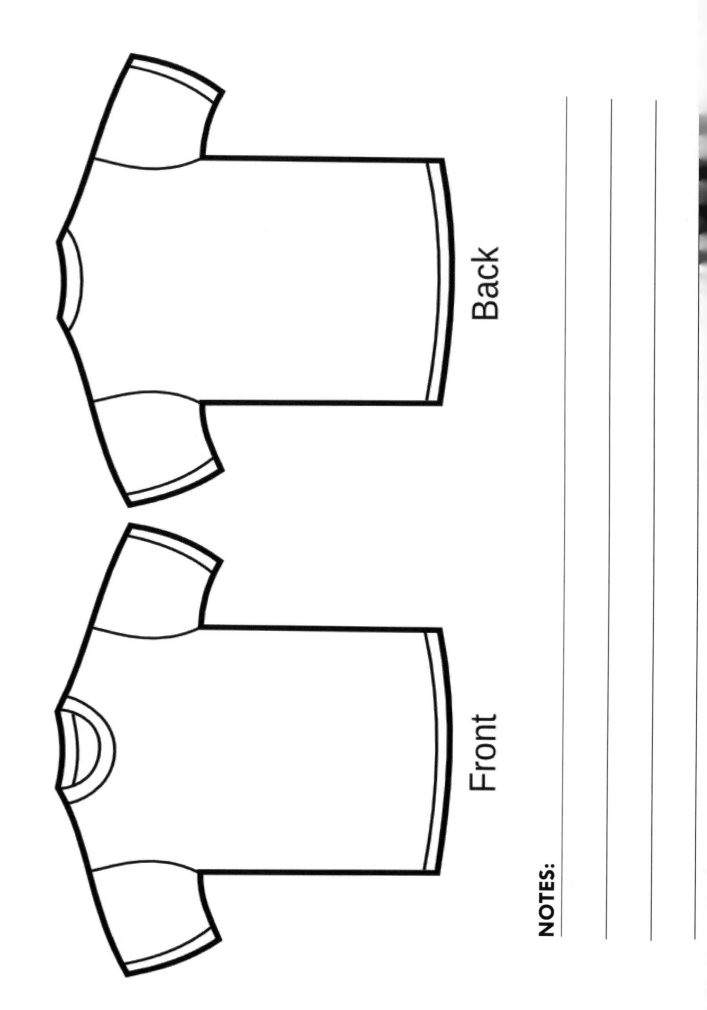

Back

Front

NOTES:

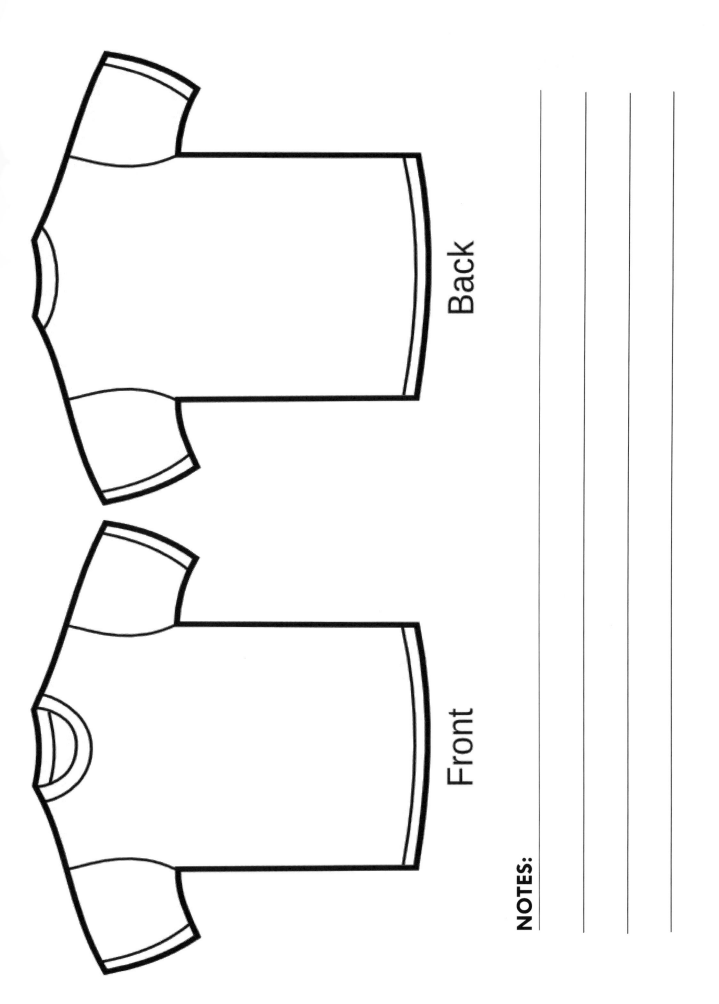

Back

Front

NOTES:

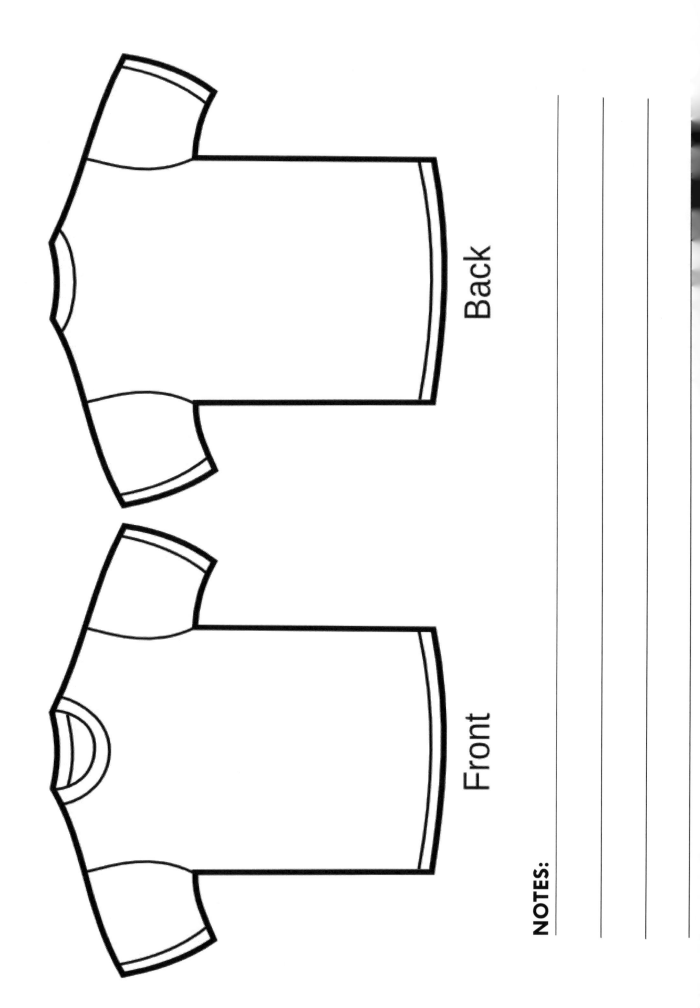

Back

Front

NOTES:

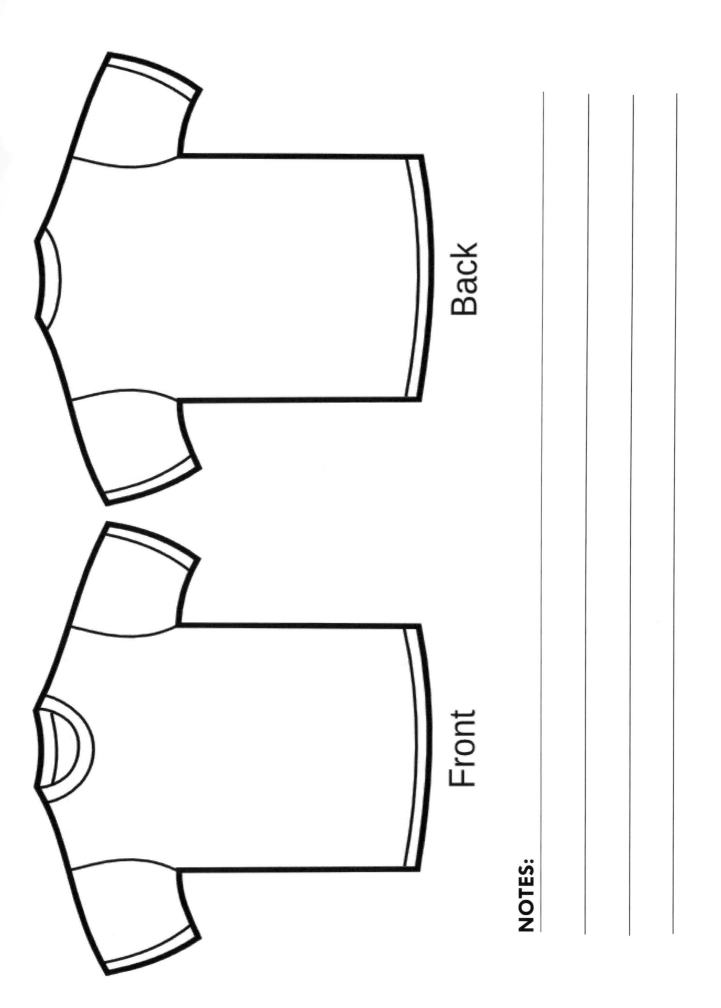

Back

Front

NOTES:

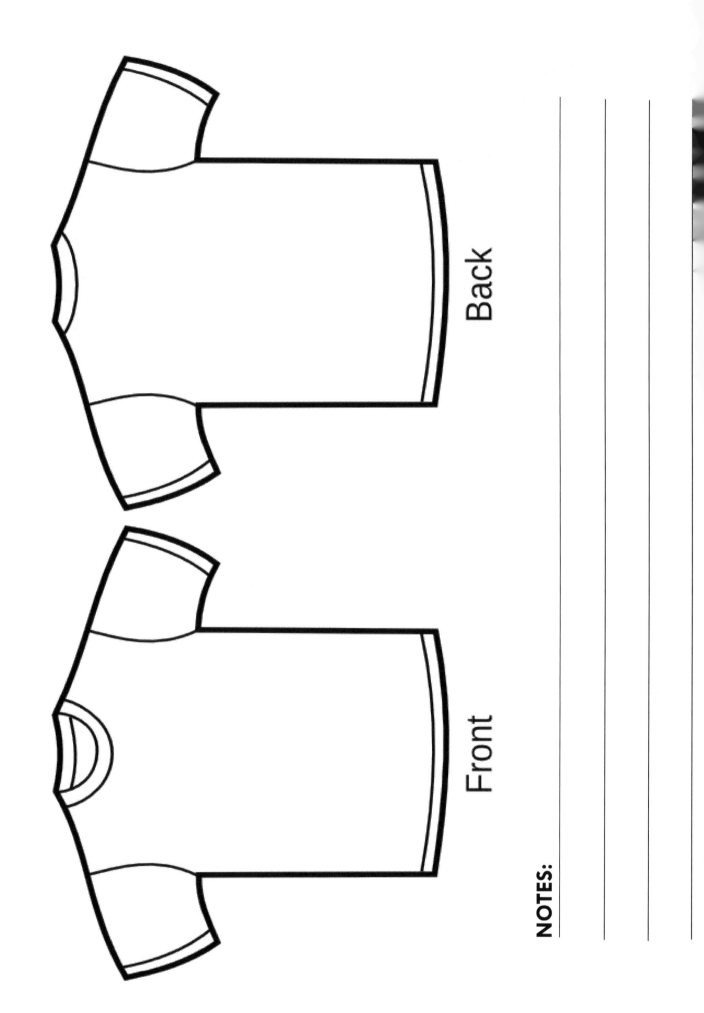

Back

Front

NOTES:

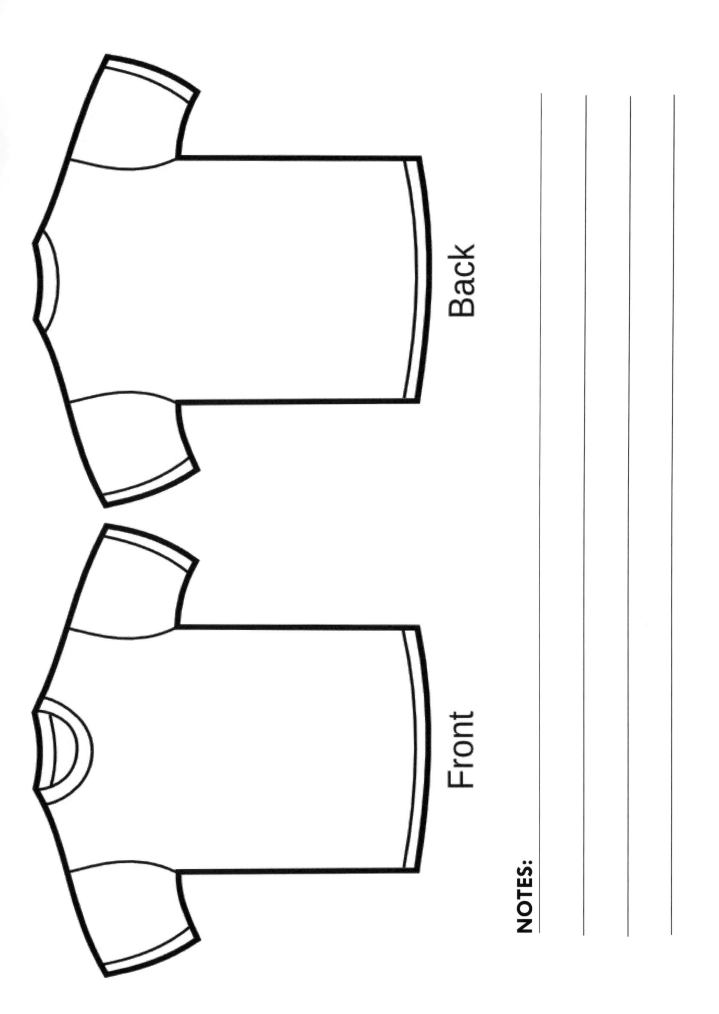

Back

Front

NOTES:

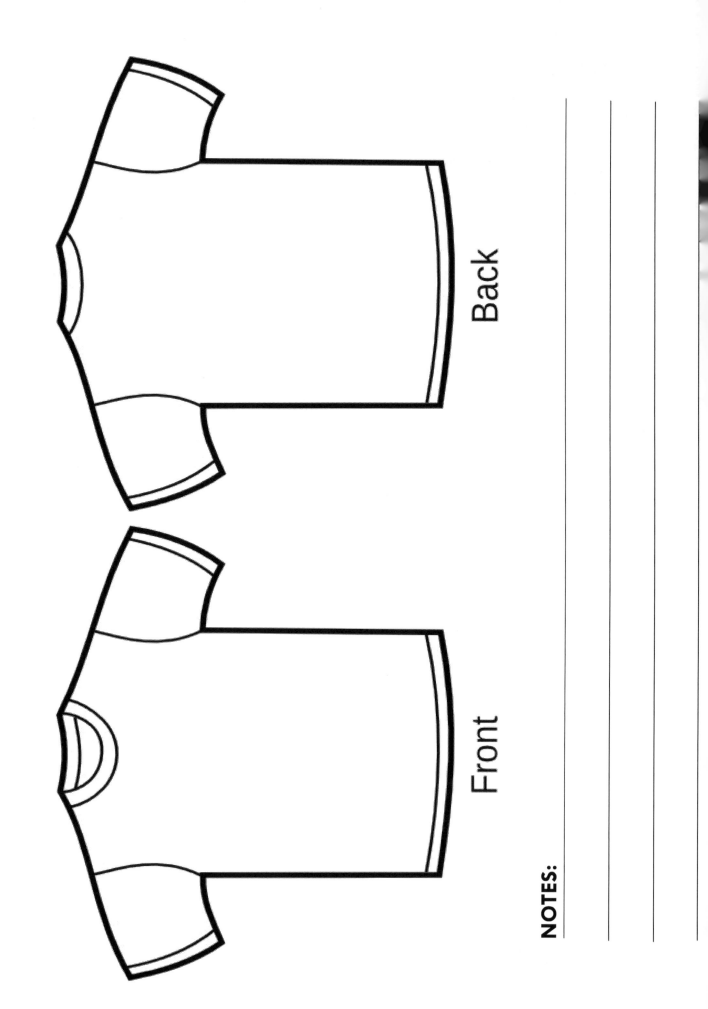

Back

Front

NOTES:

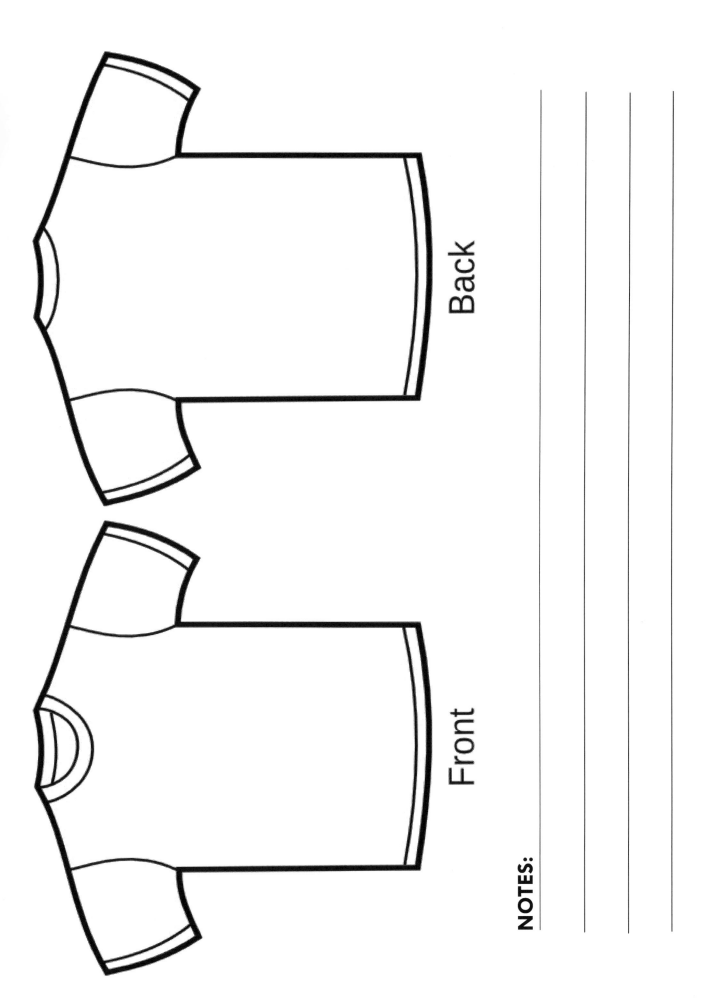

Back

Front

NOTES:

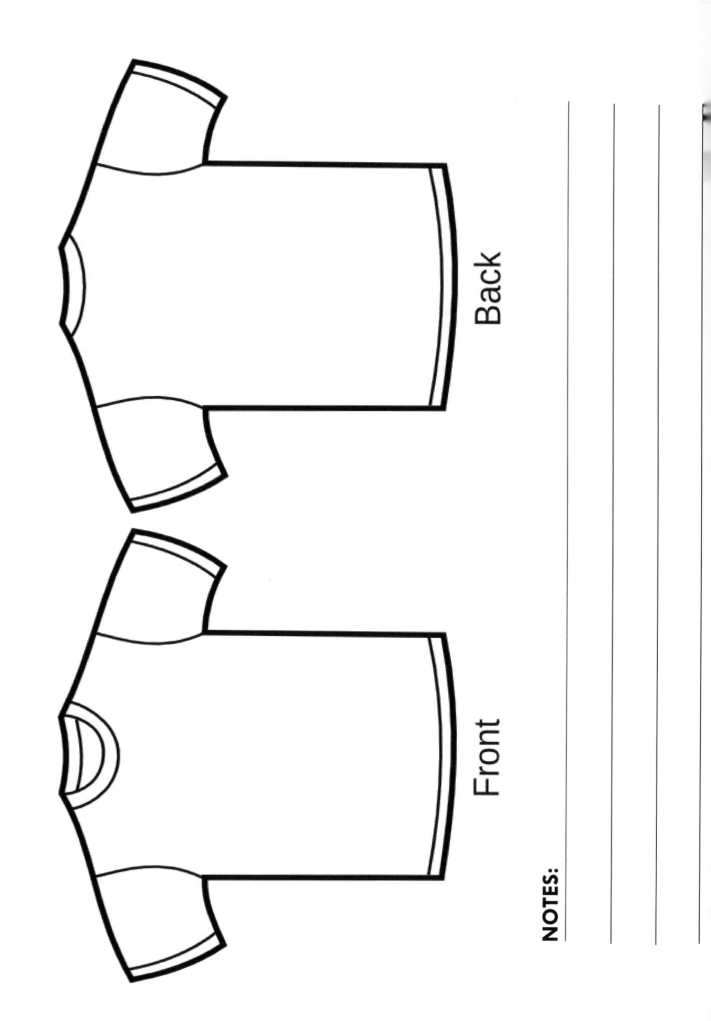

Back

Front

NOTES:

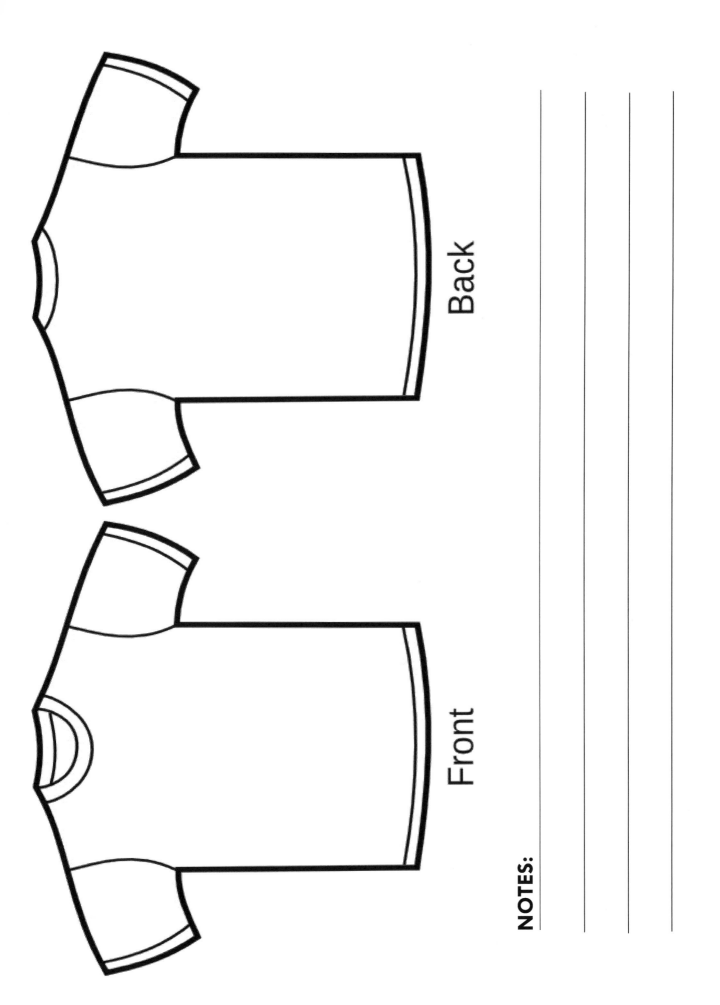

Front

Back

NOTES:

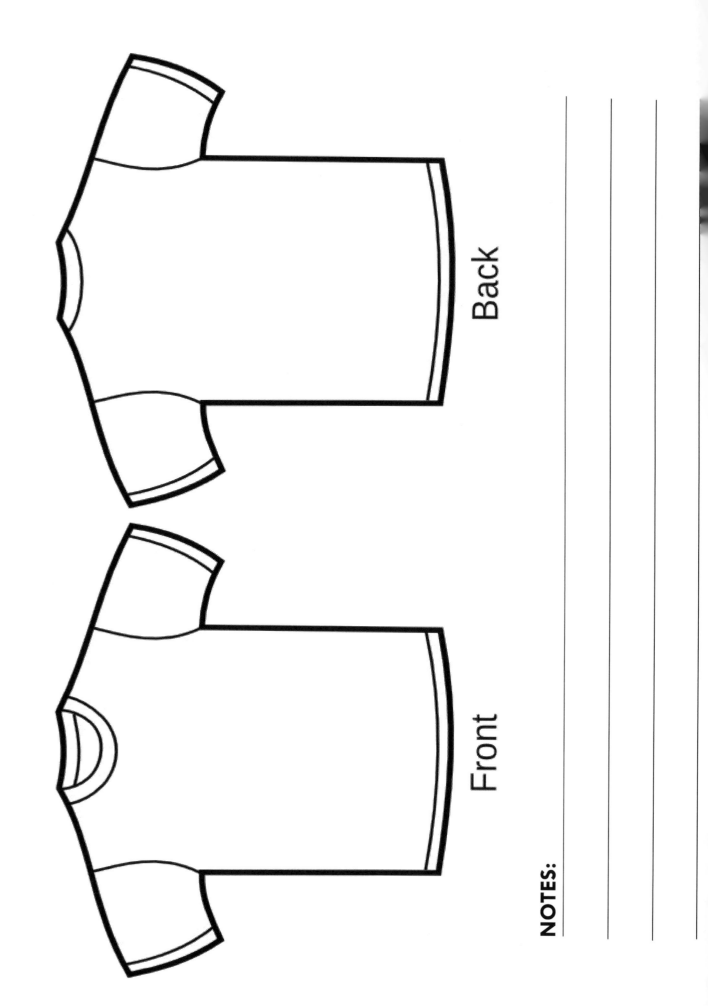

Back

Front

NOTES:

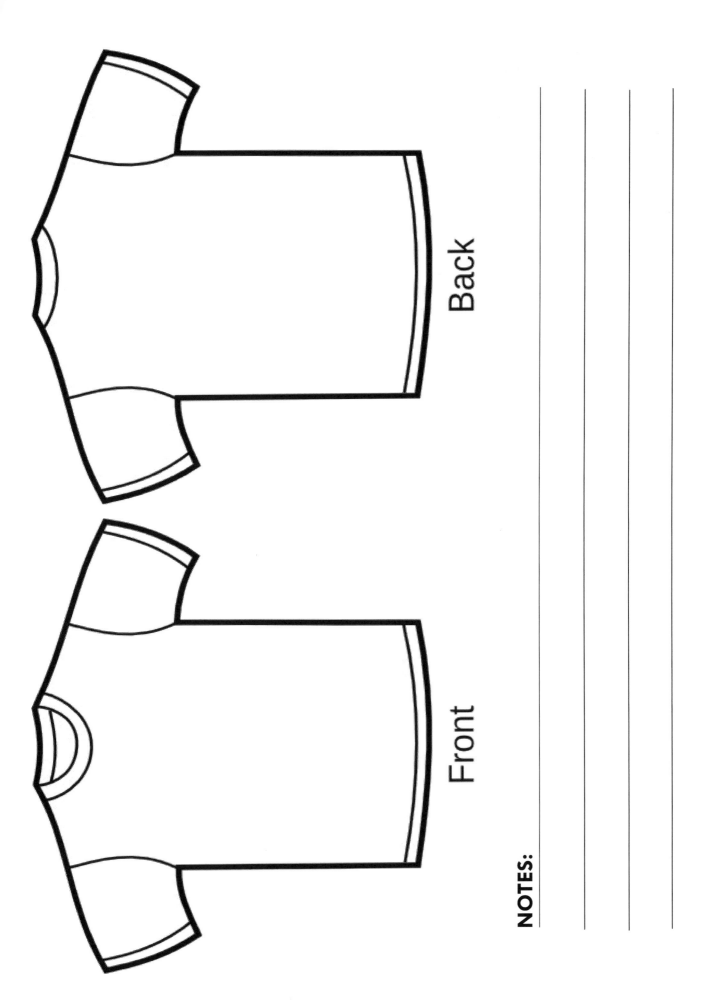

Back

Front

NOTES:

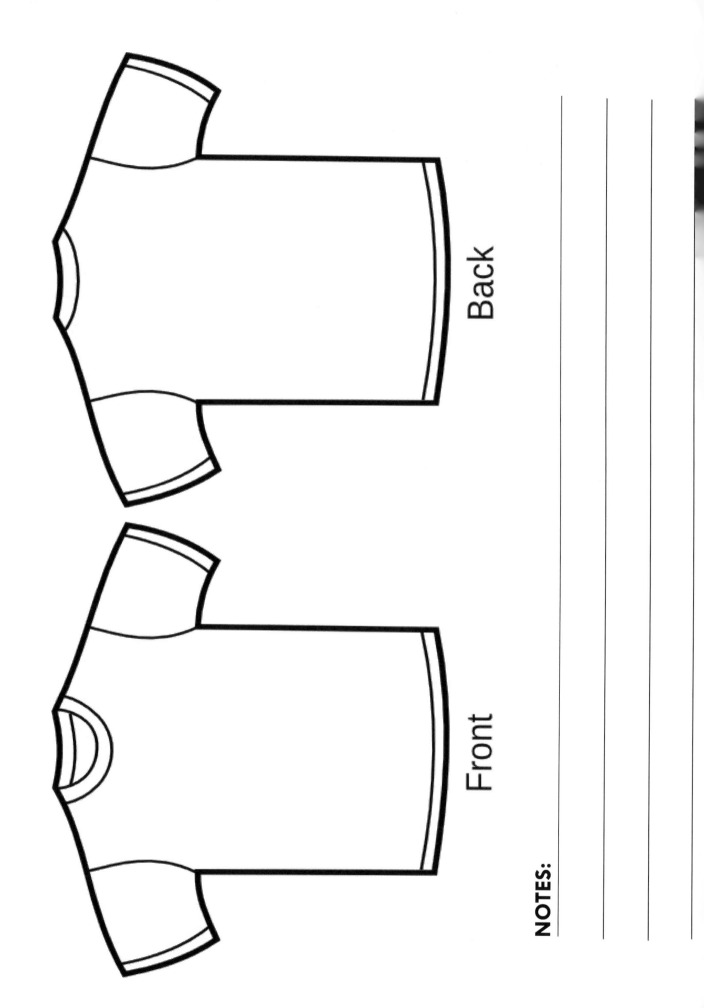

Back

Front

NOTES:

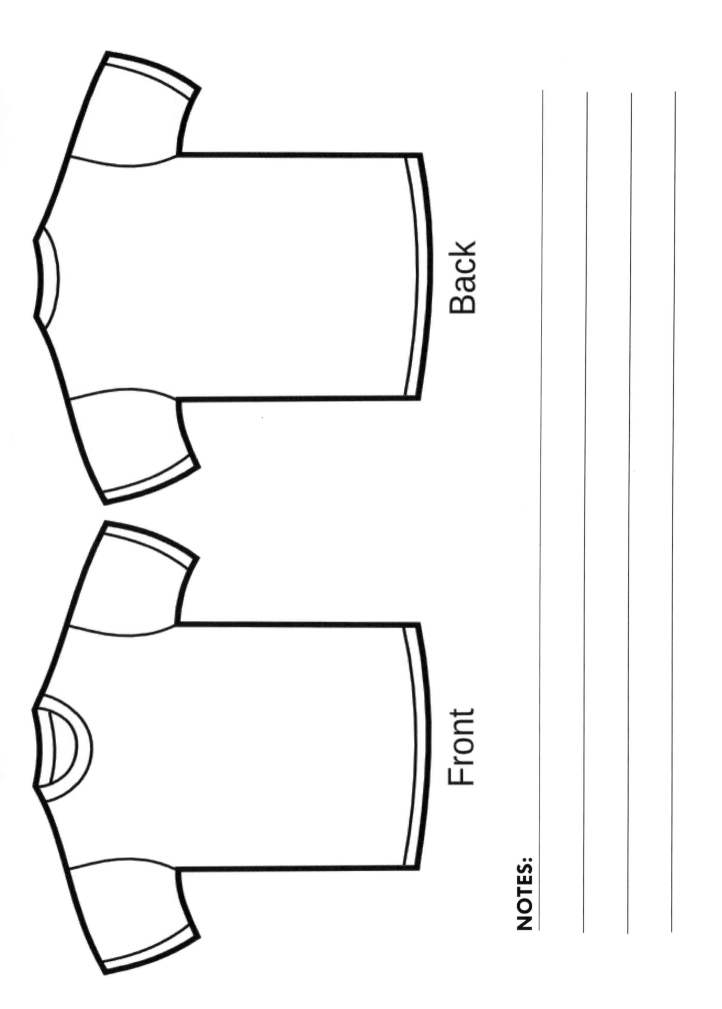

Back

Front

NOTES:

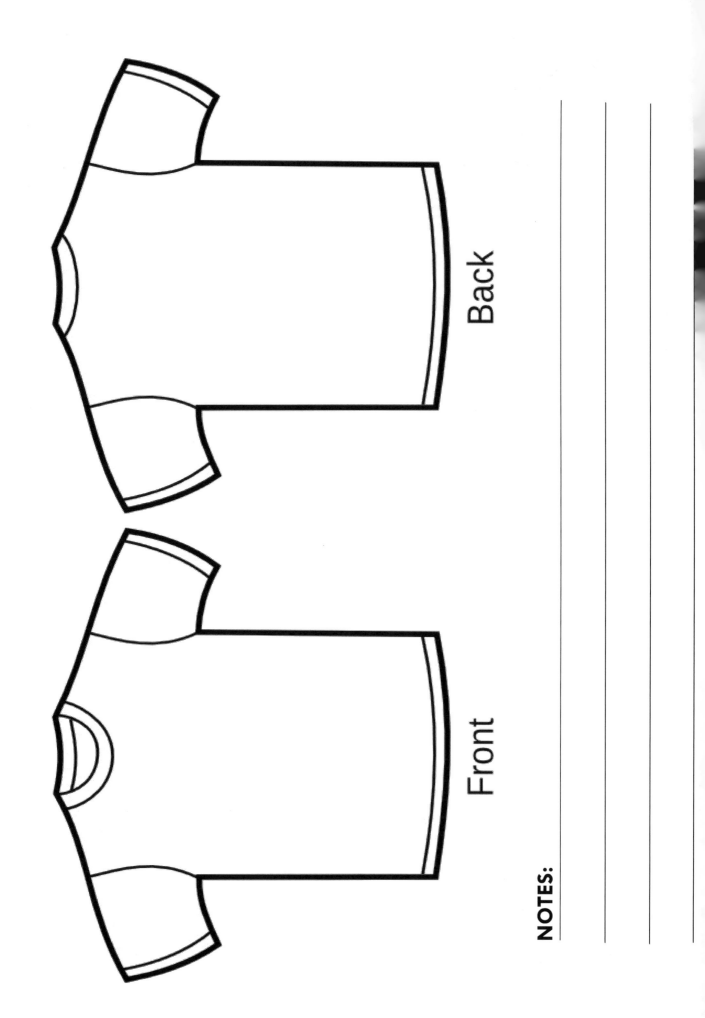

Back

Front

NOTES:

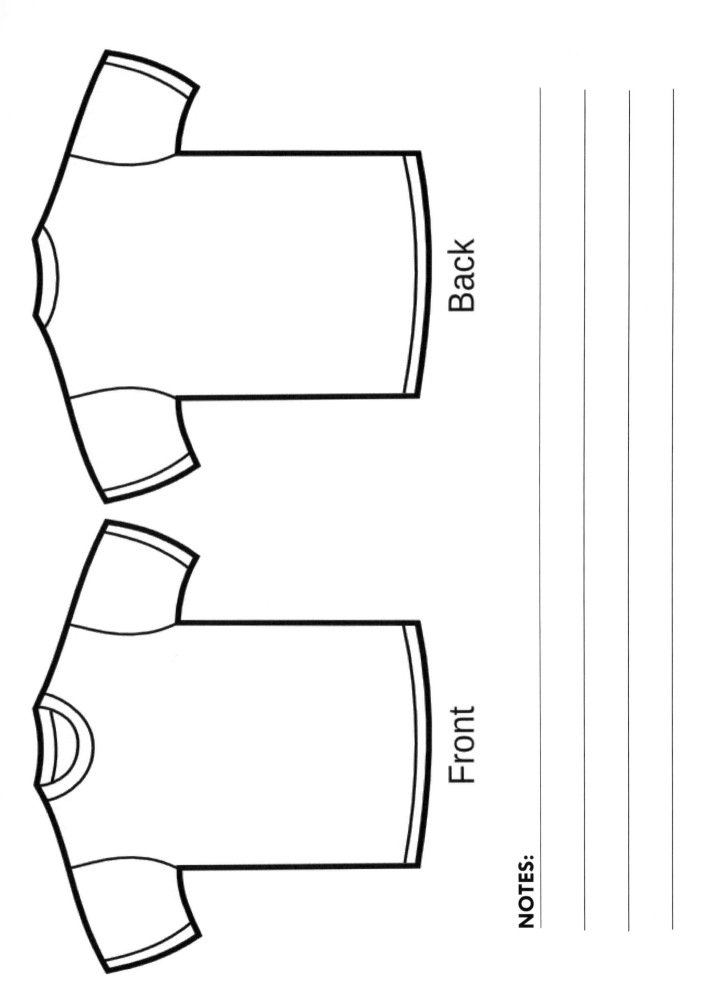

Back

Front

NOTES:

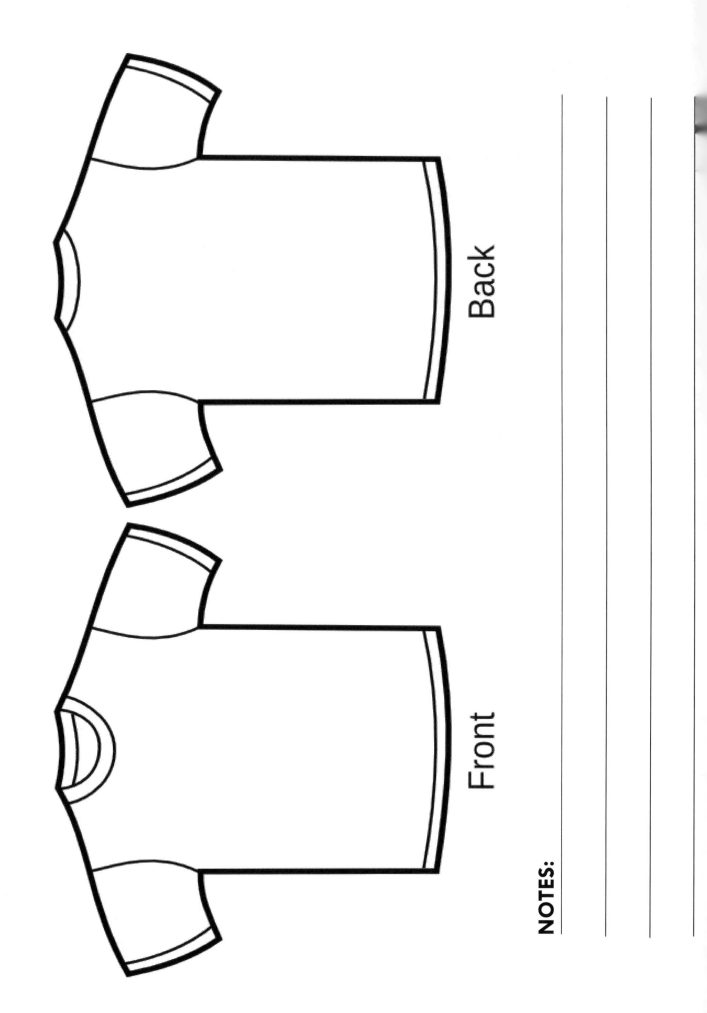

Back

Front

NOTES:

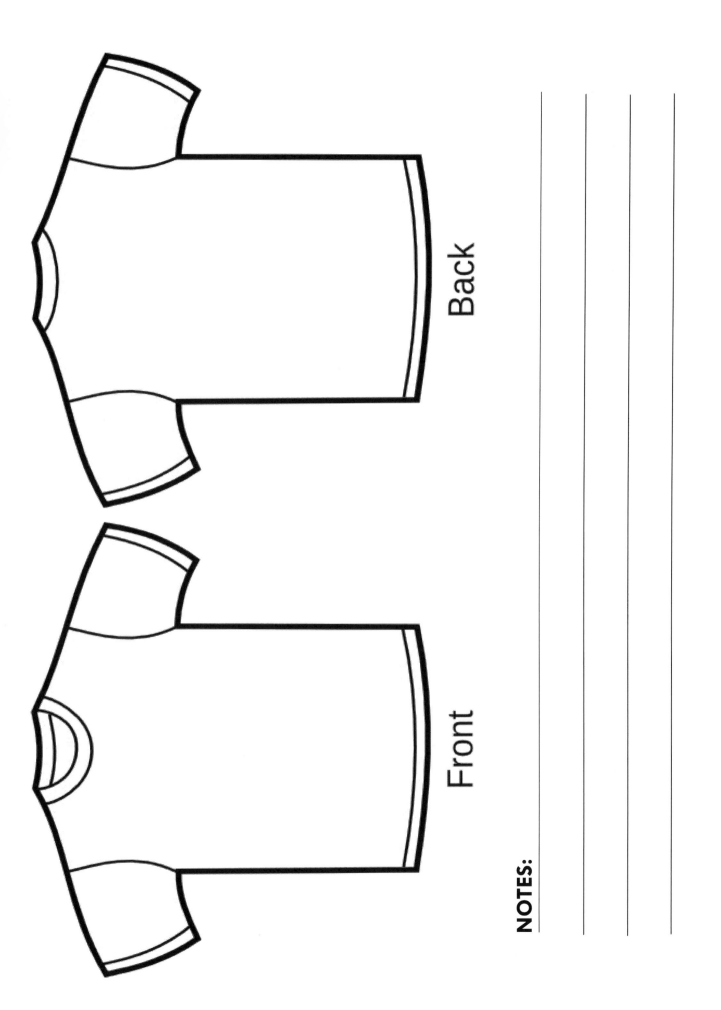

Back

Front

NOTES:

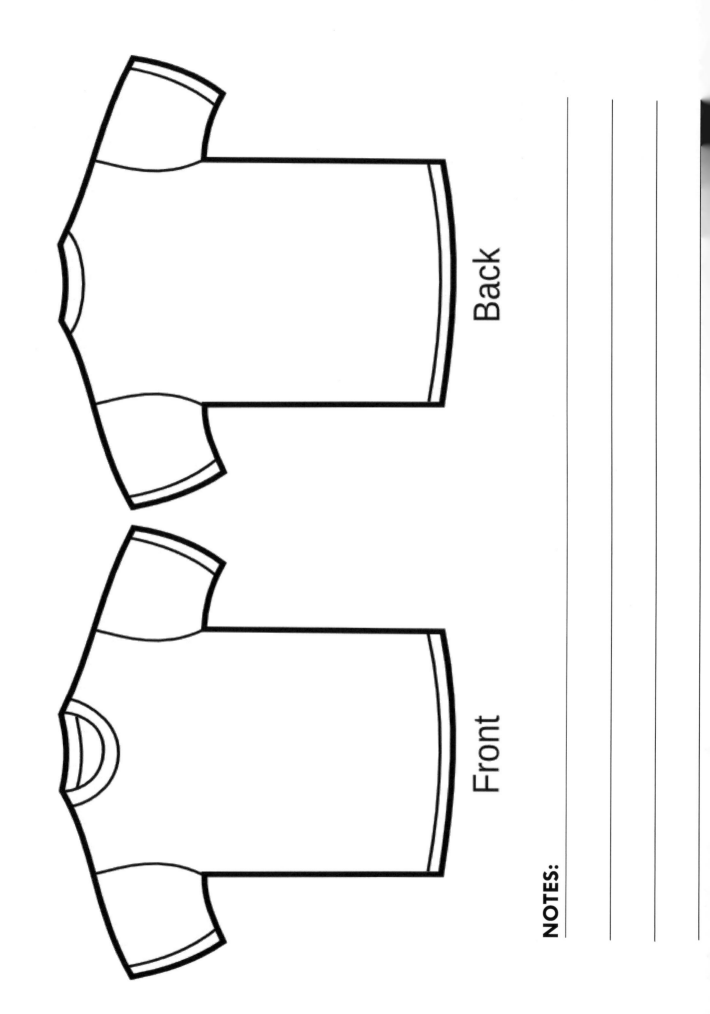

Back

Front

NOTES:

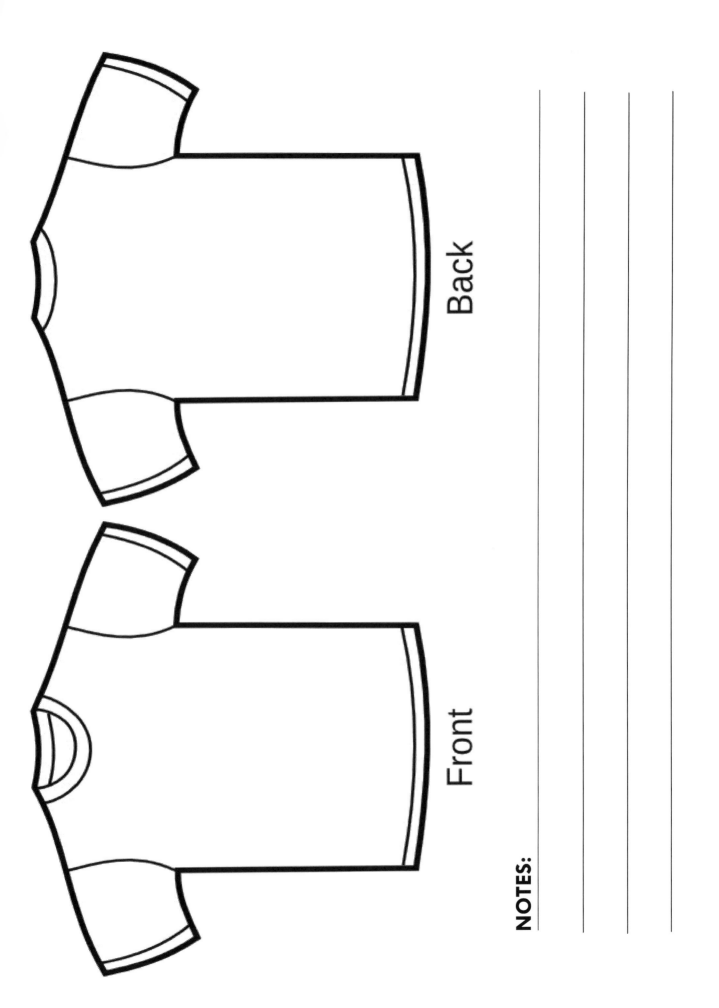

Back

Front

NOTES:

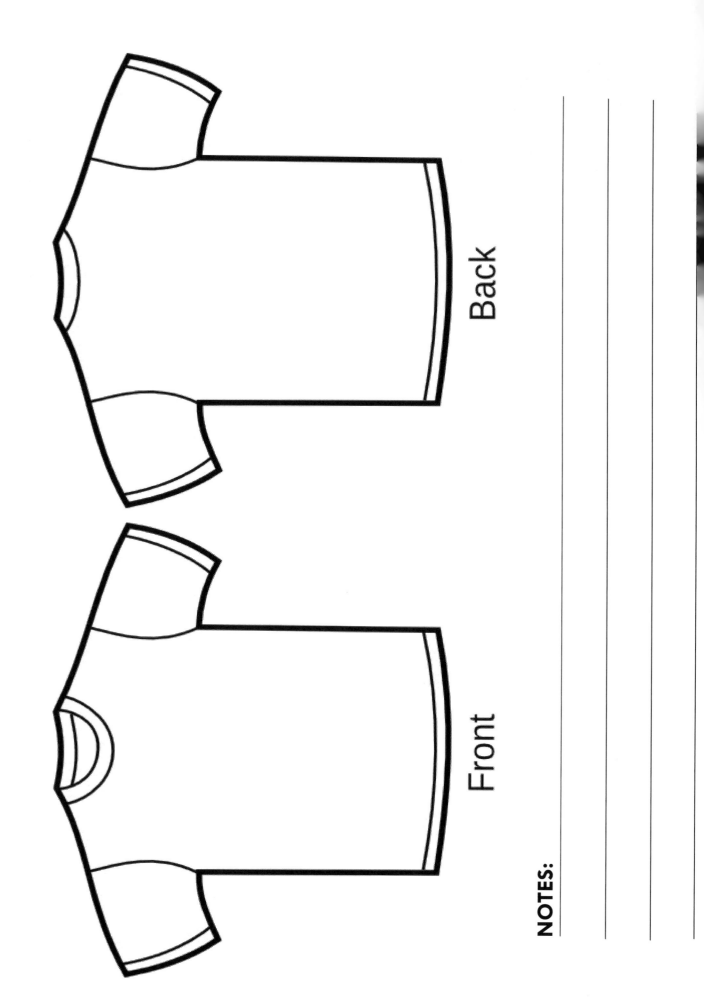

Back

Front

NOTES:

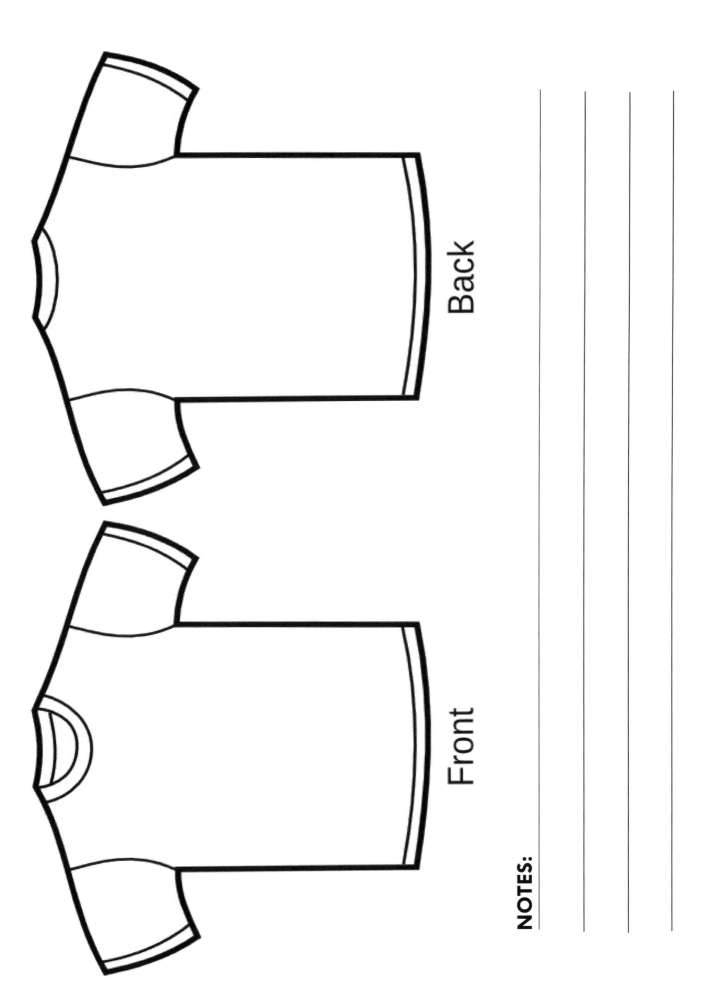

Back

Front

NOTES:

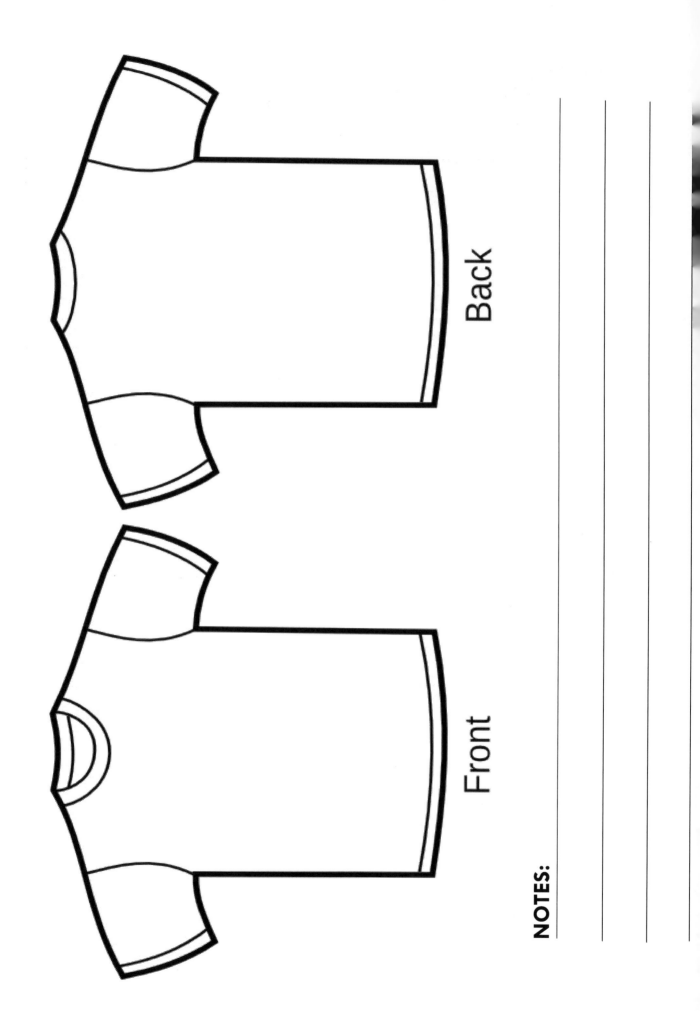

Back

Front

NOTES:

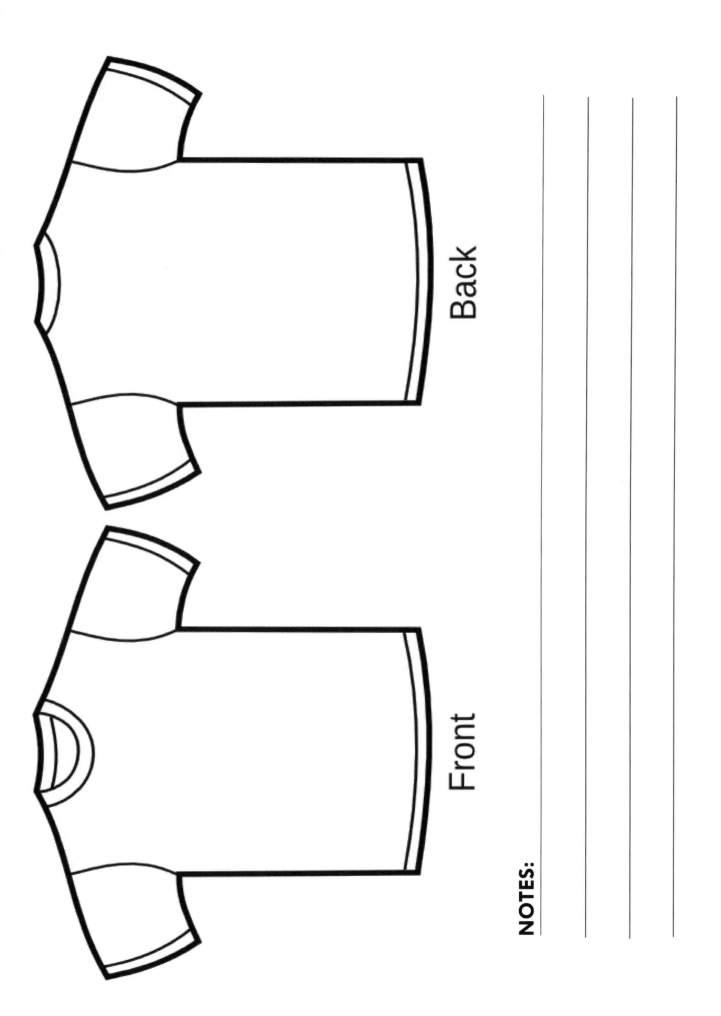

Back

Front

NOTES:

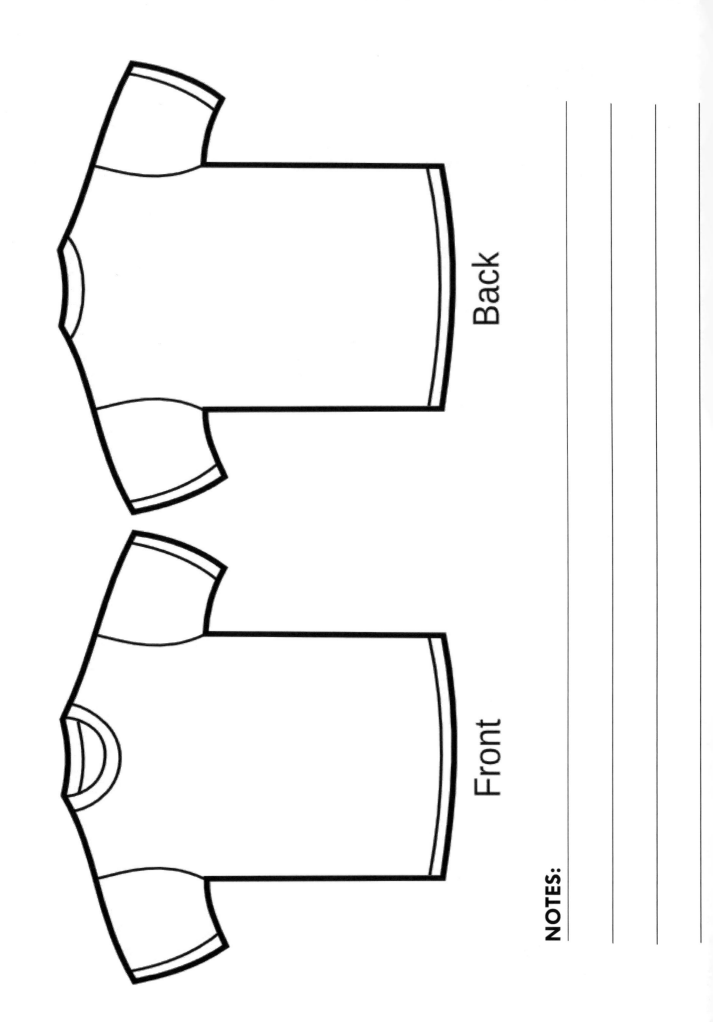

Back

Front

NOTES:

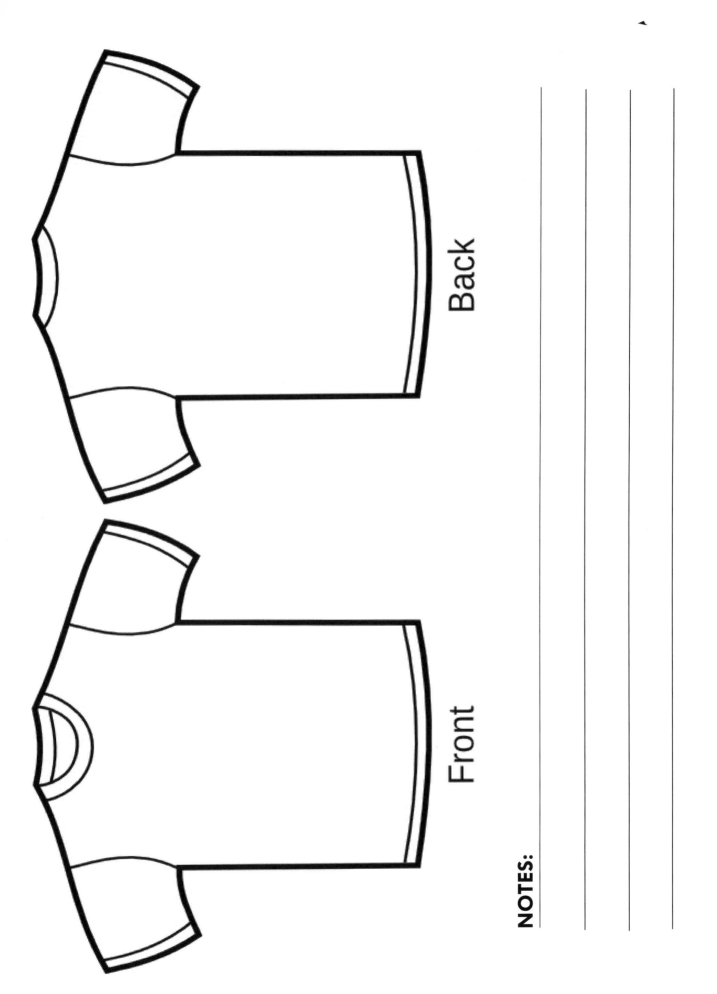

Back

Front

NOTES:

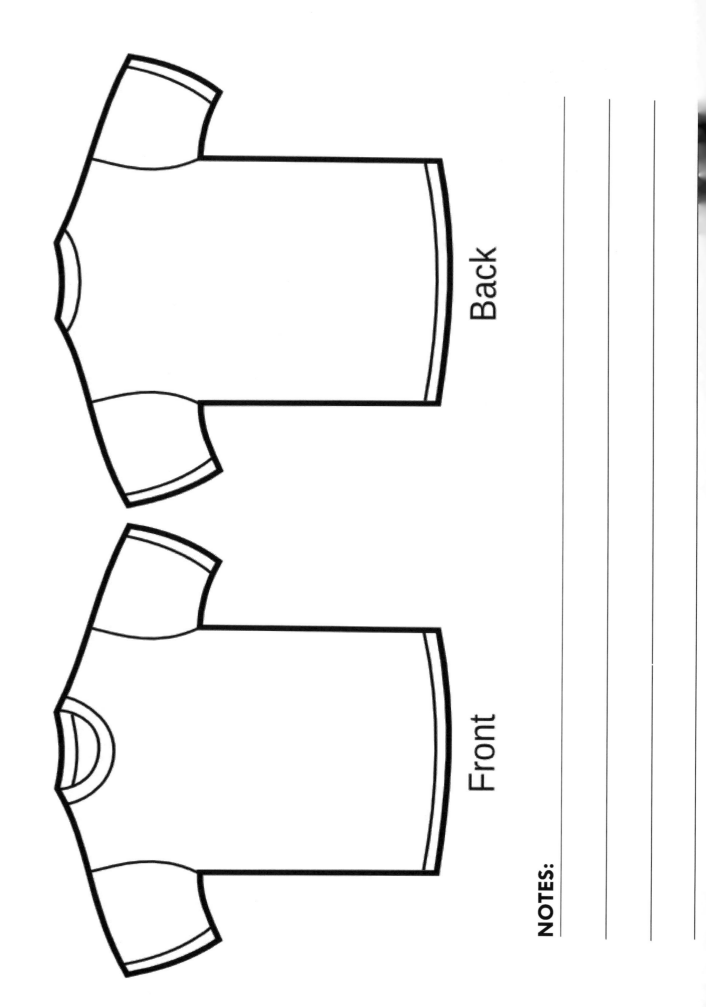

Back

Front

NOTES:

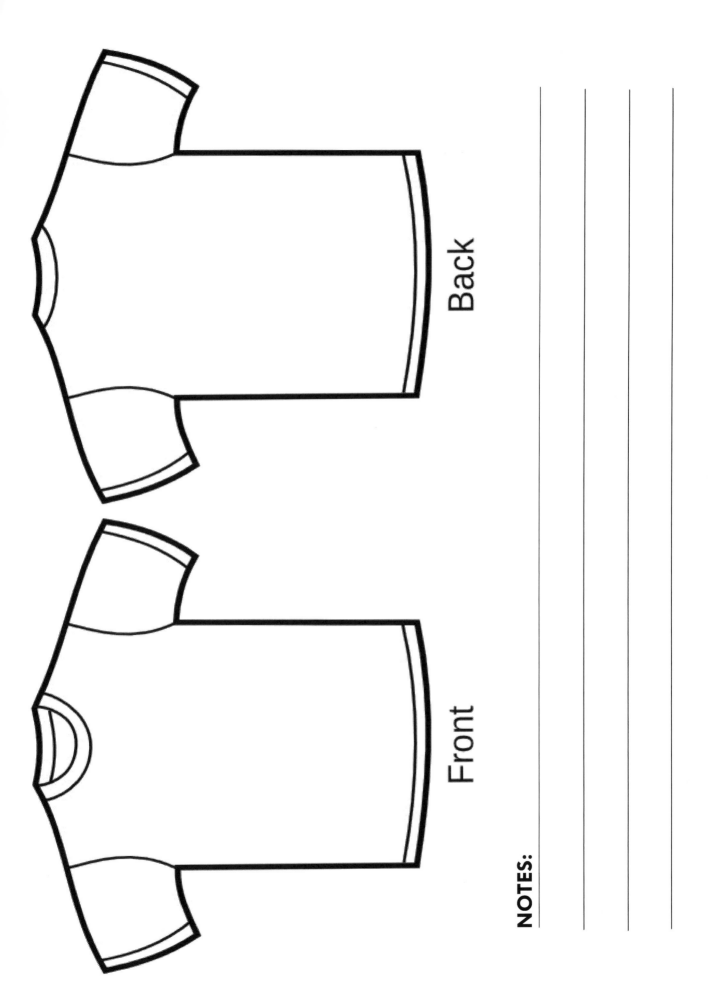

Back

Front

NOTES:

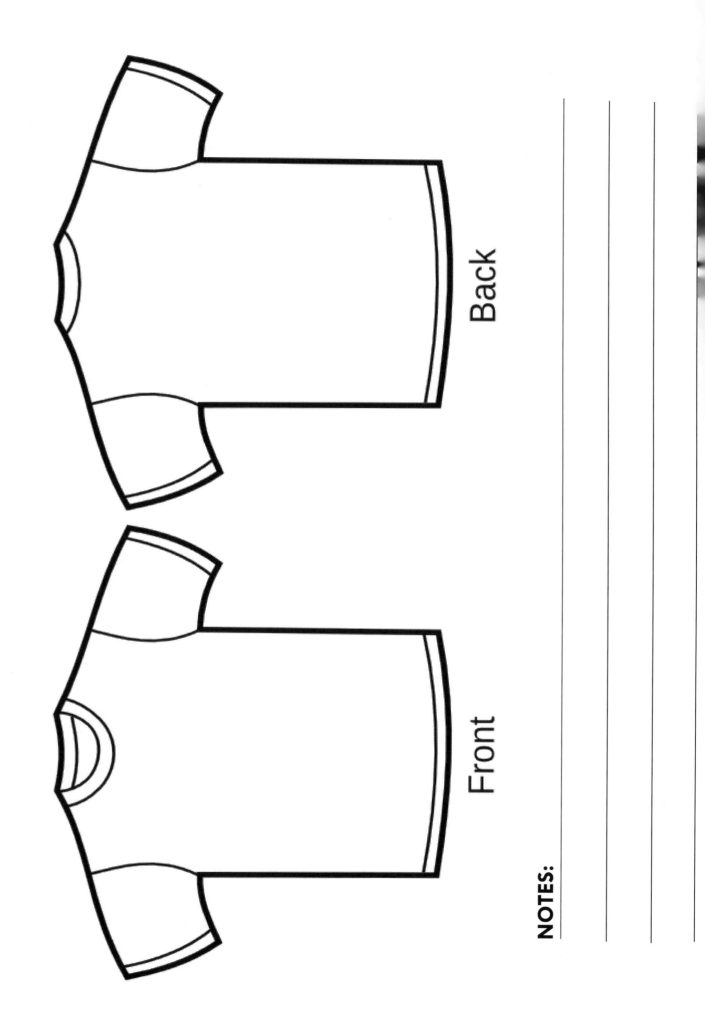

Back

Front

NOTES:

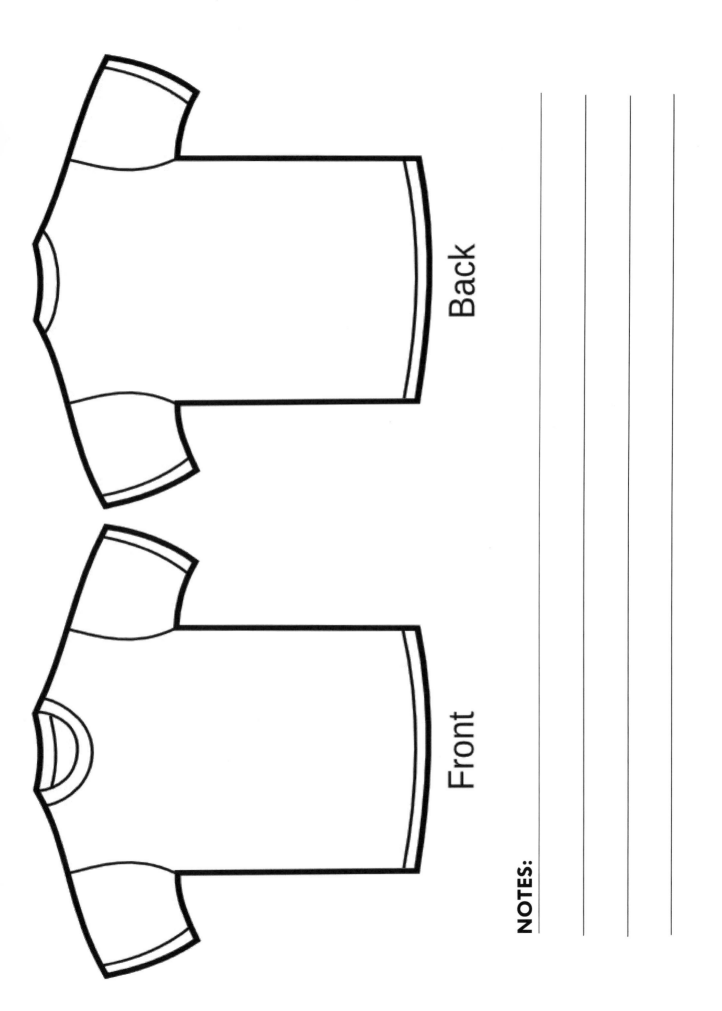

Back

Front

NOTES:

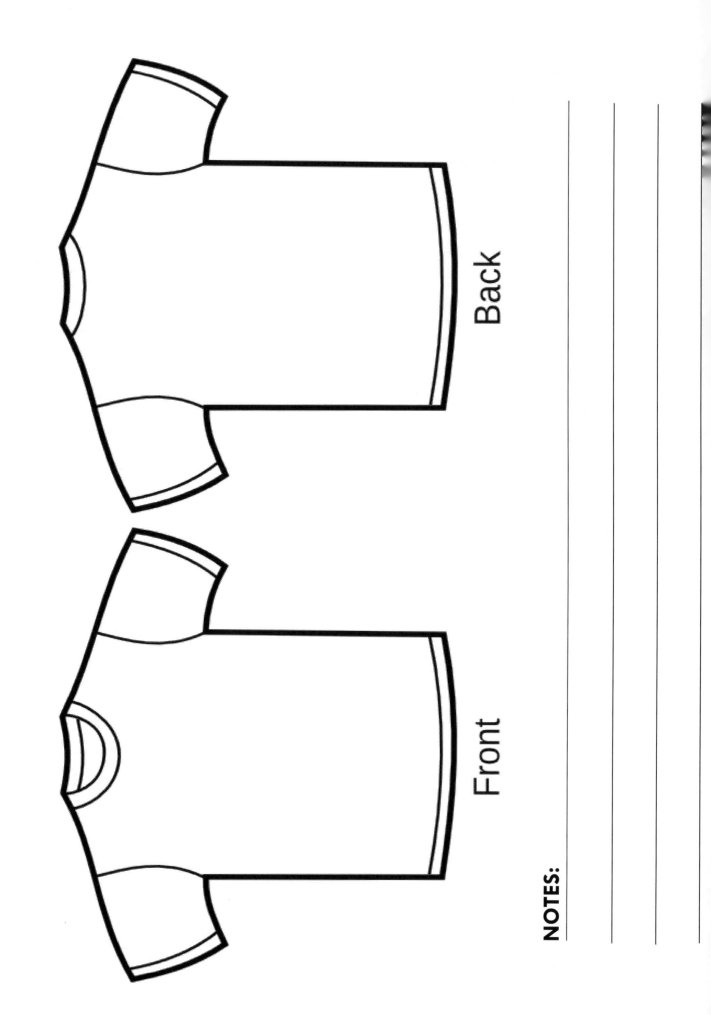

Back

Front

NOTES:

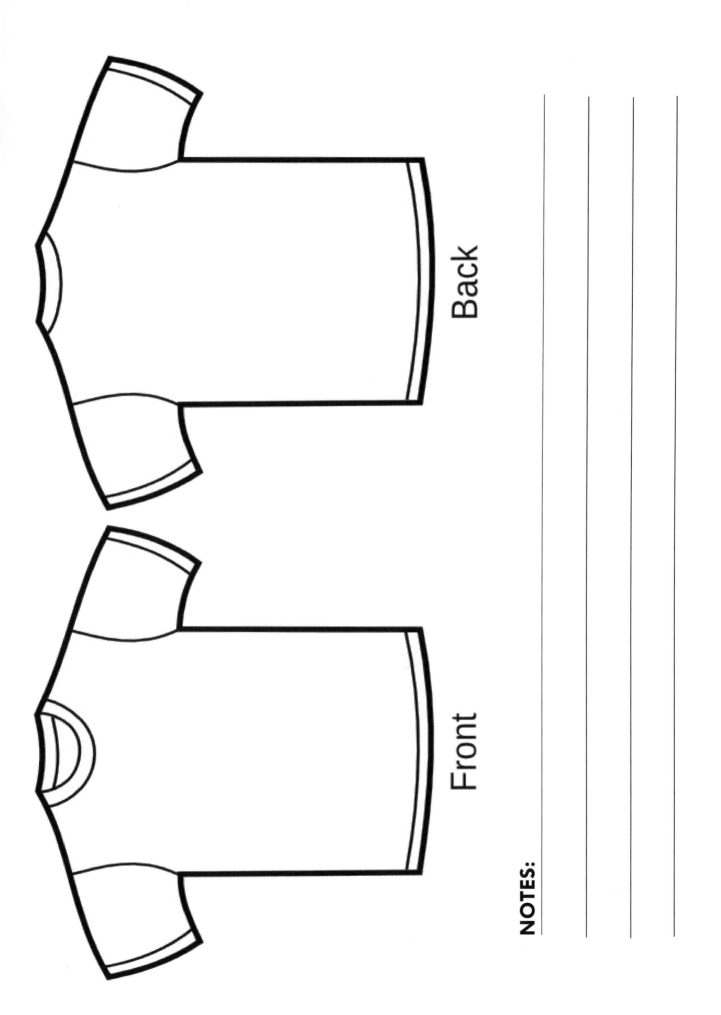

Back

Front

NOTES:

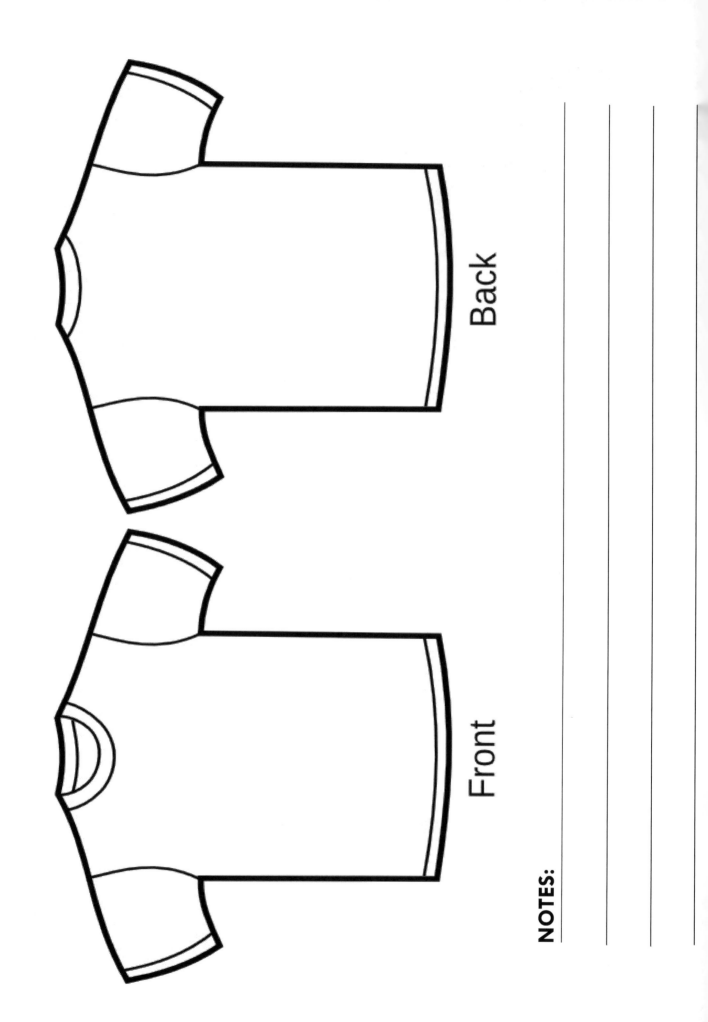

Back

Front

NOTES:

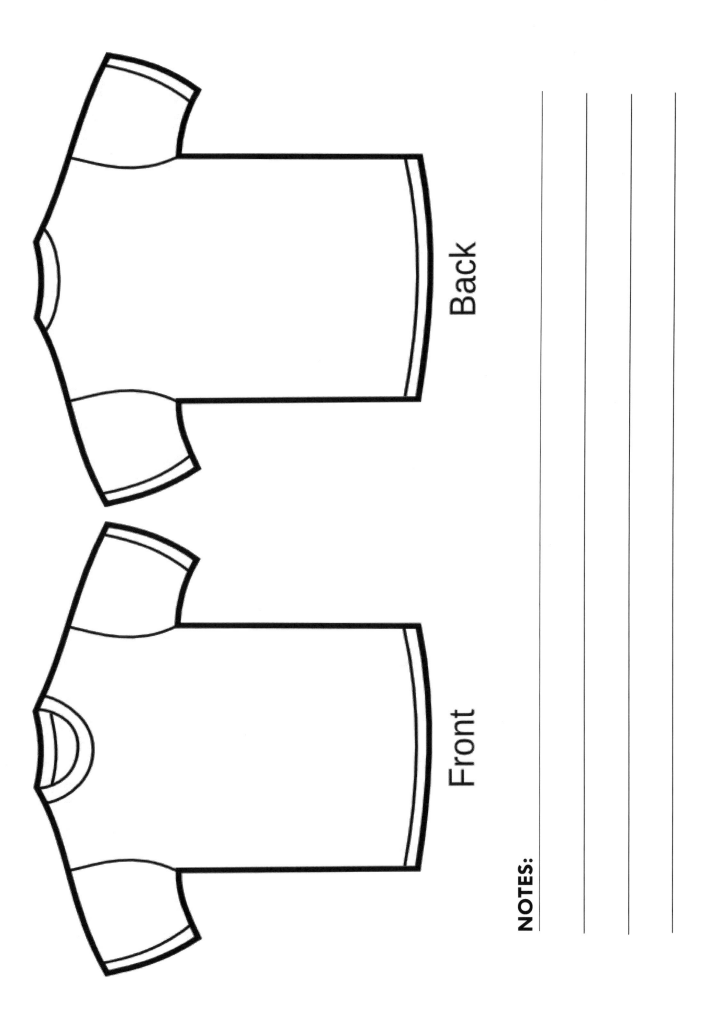

Back

Front

NOTES:

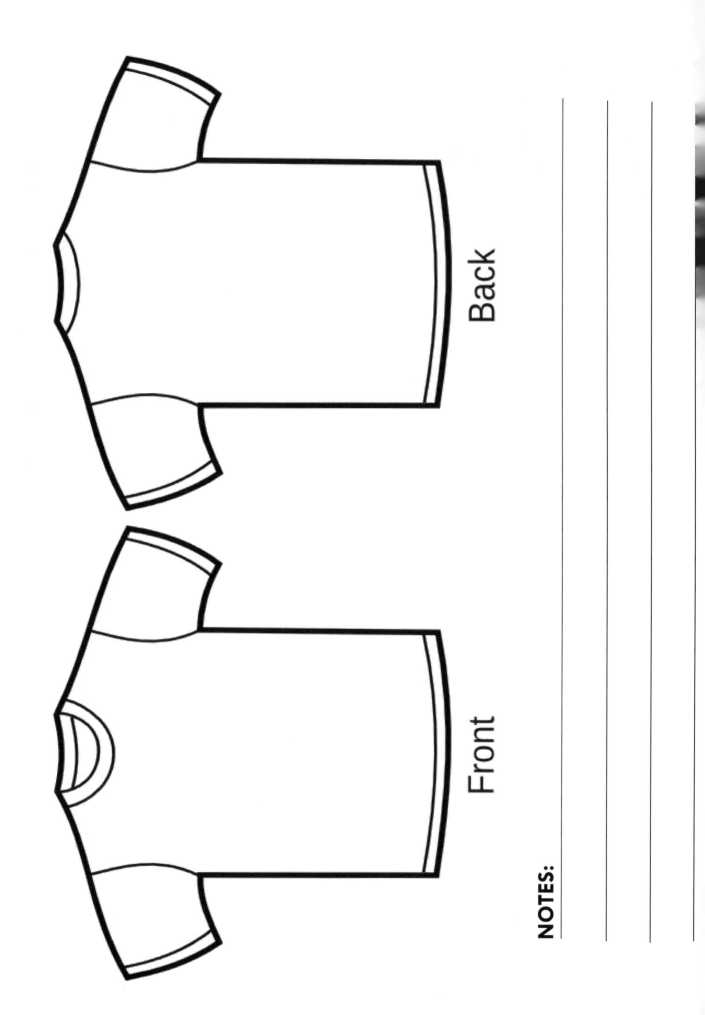

Back

Front

NOTES:

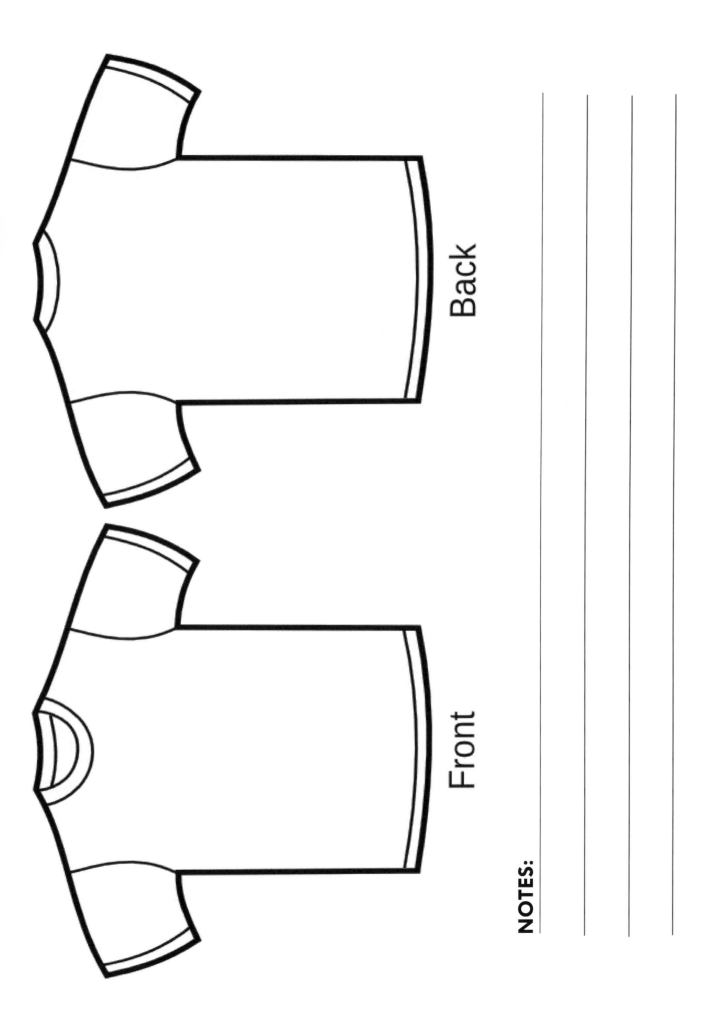

Back

Front

NOTES:

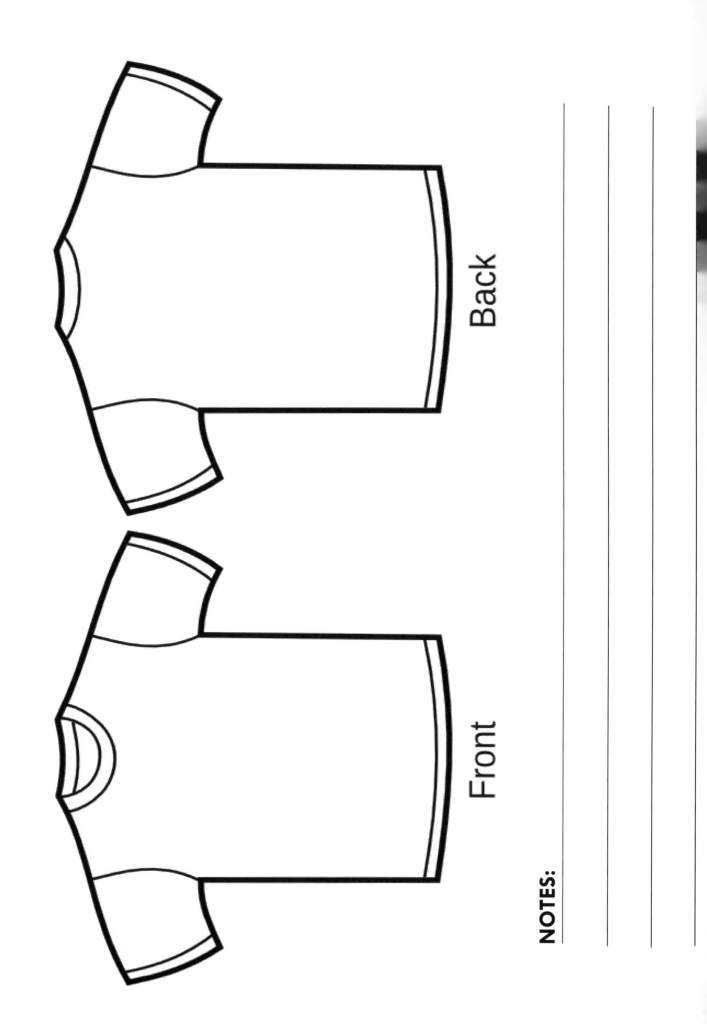

Back

Front

NOTES:

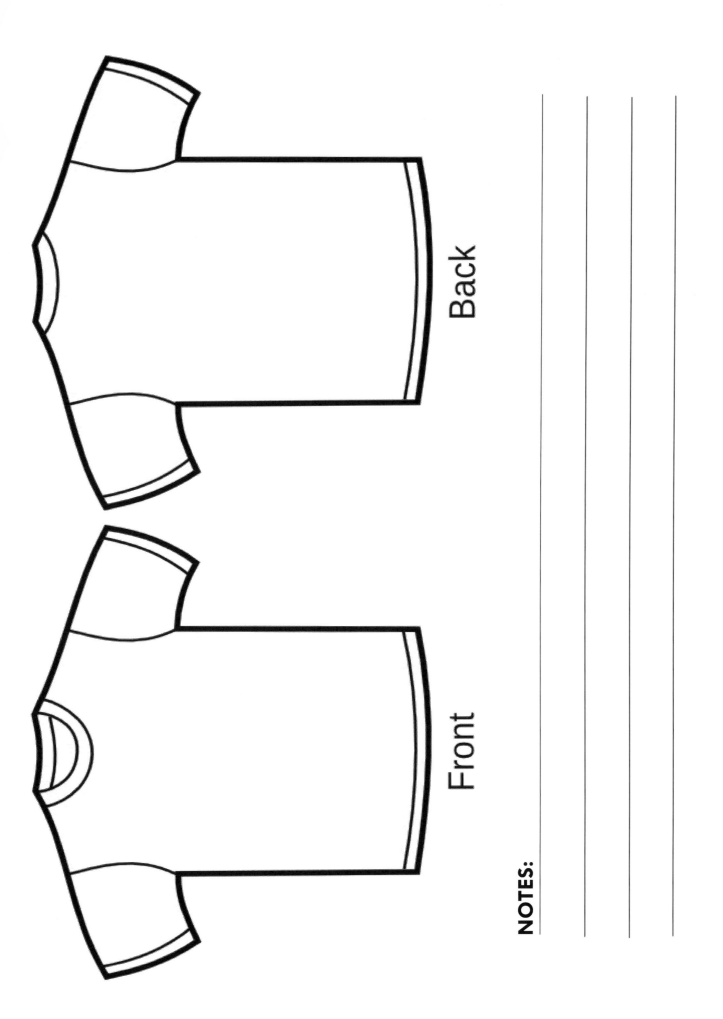

Back

Front

NOTES:

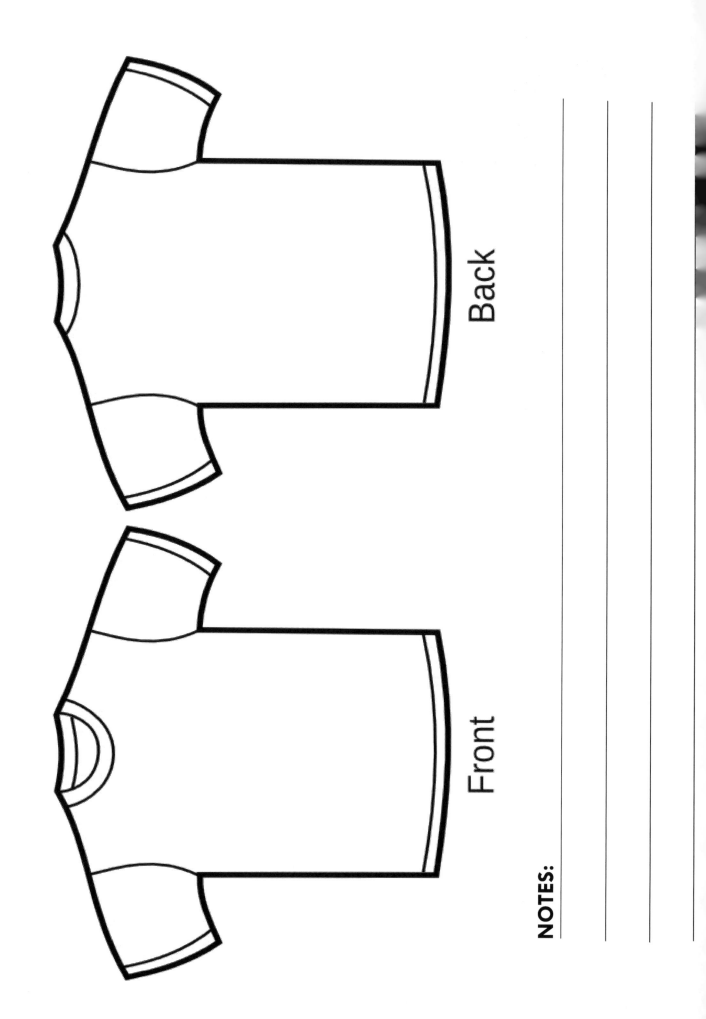

Back

Front

NOTES:

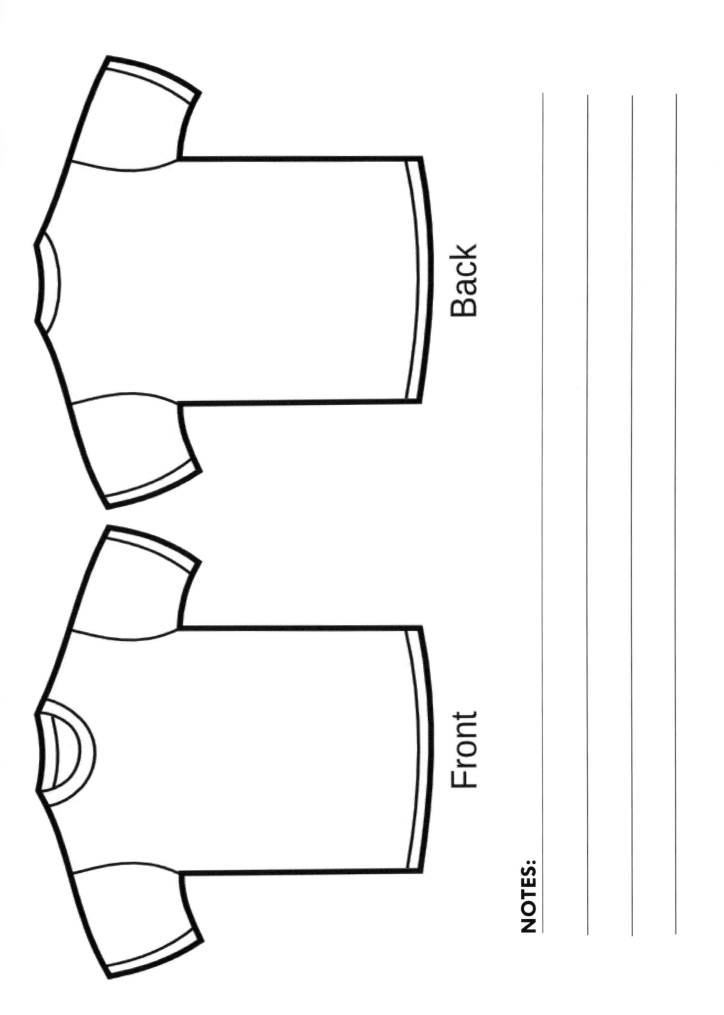

Back

Front

NOTES:

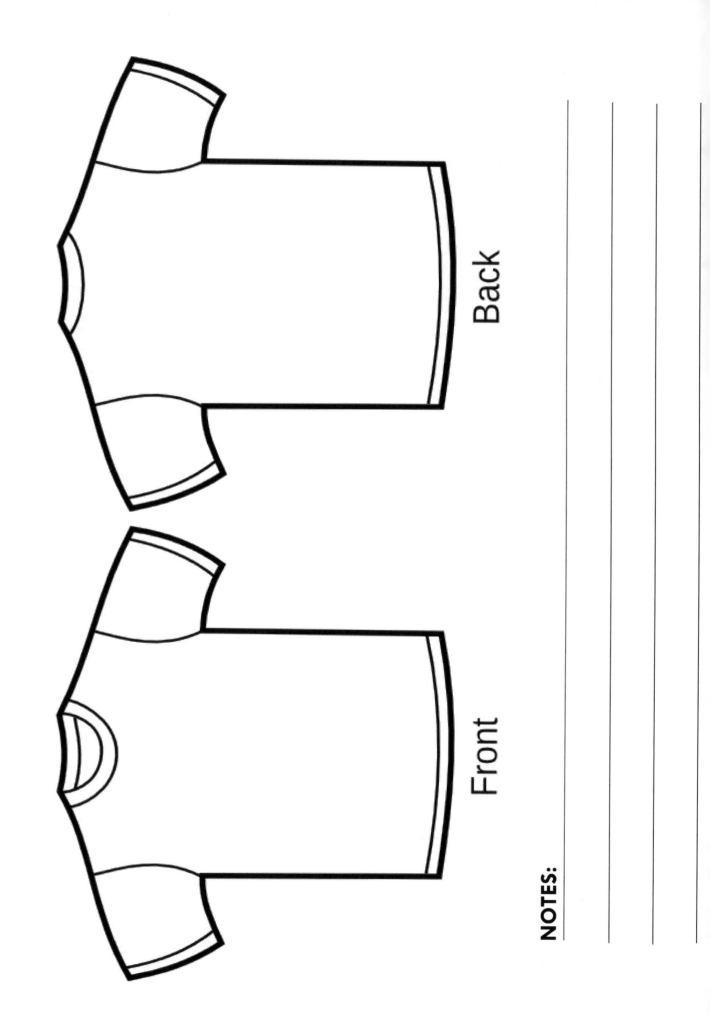

Back

Front

NOTES:

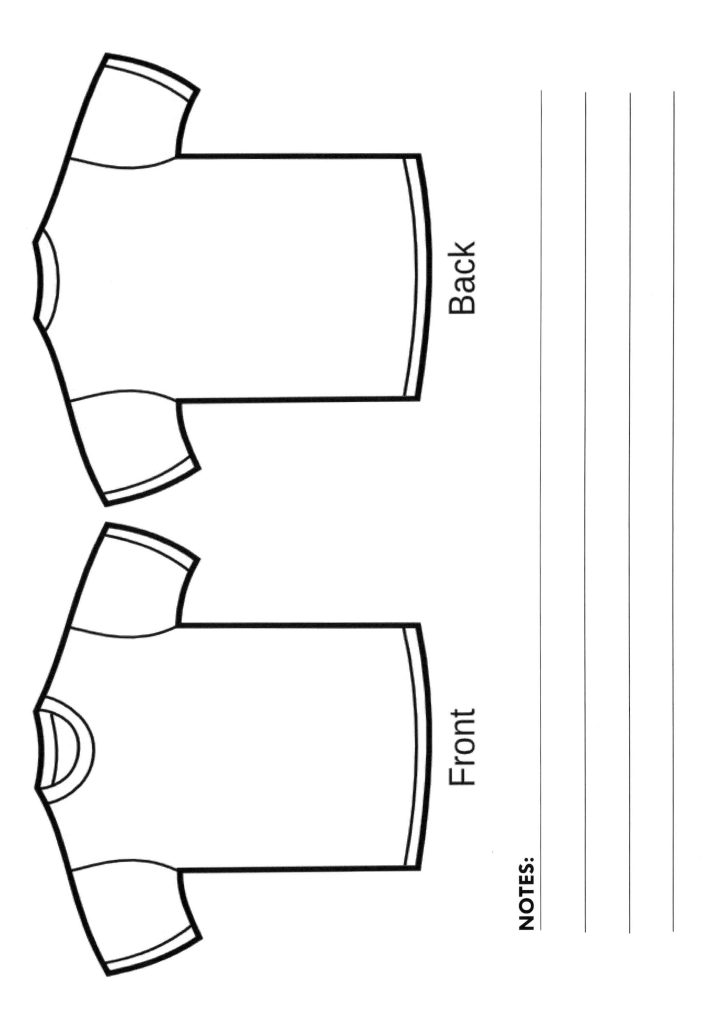

Back

Front

NOTES:

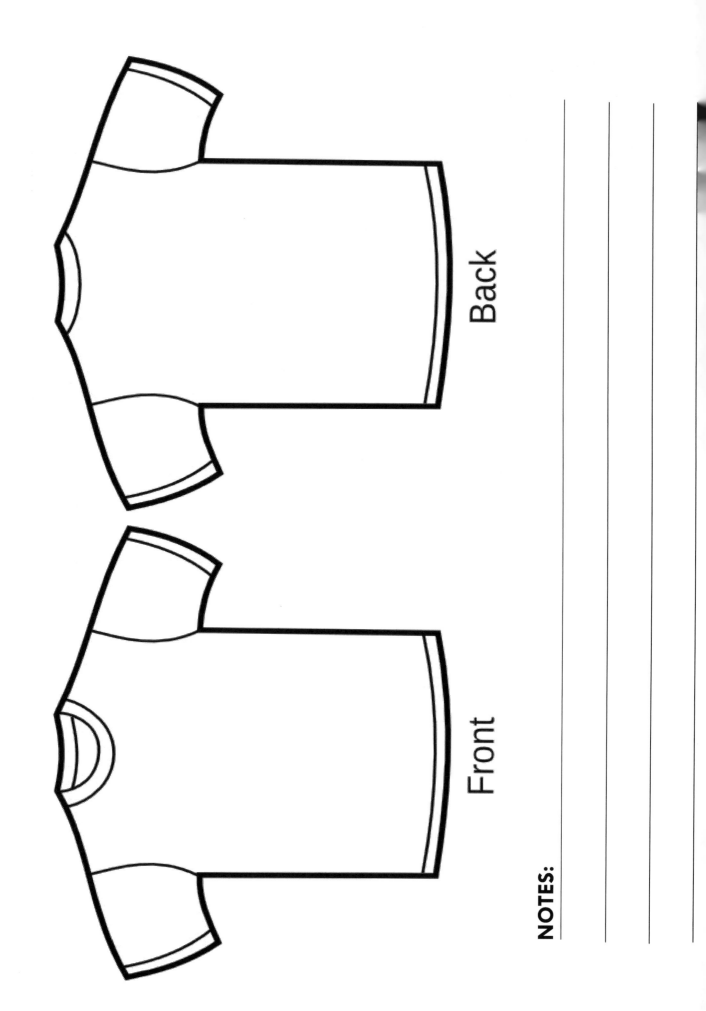

Back

Front

NOTES:

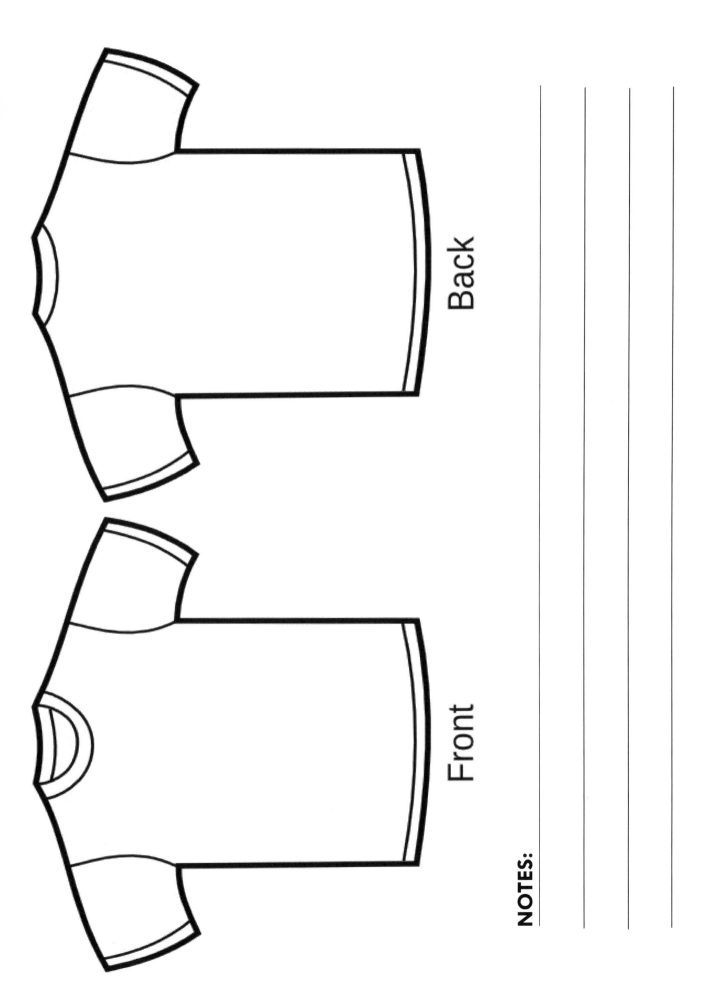

Back

Front

NOTES:

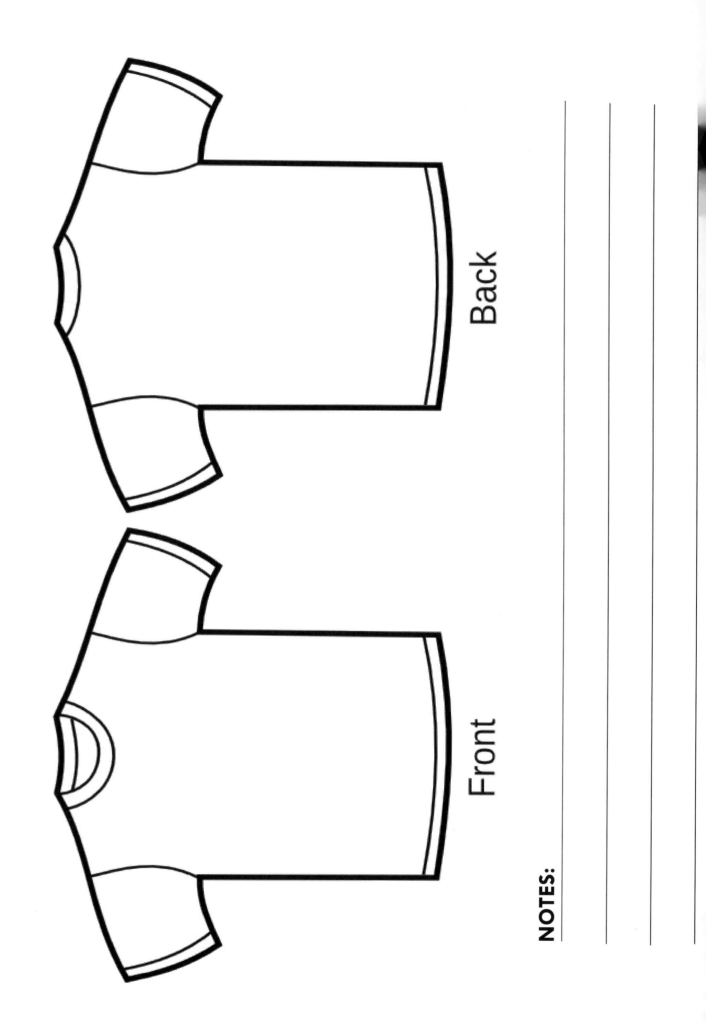

Back

Front

NOTES:

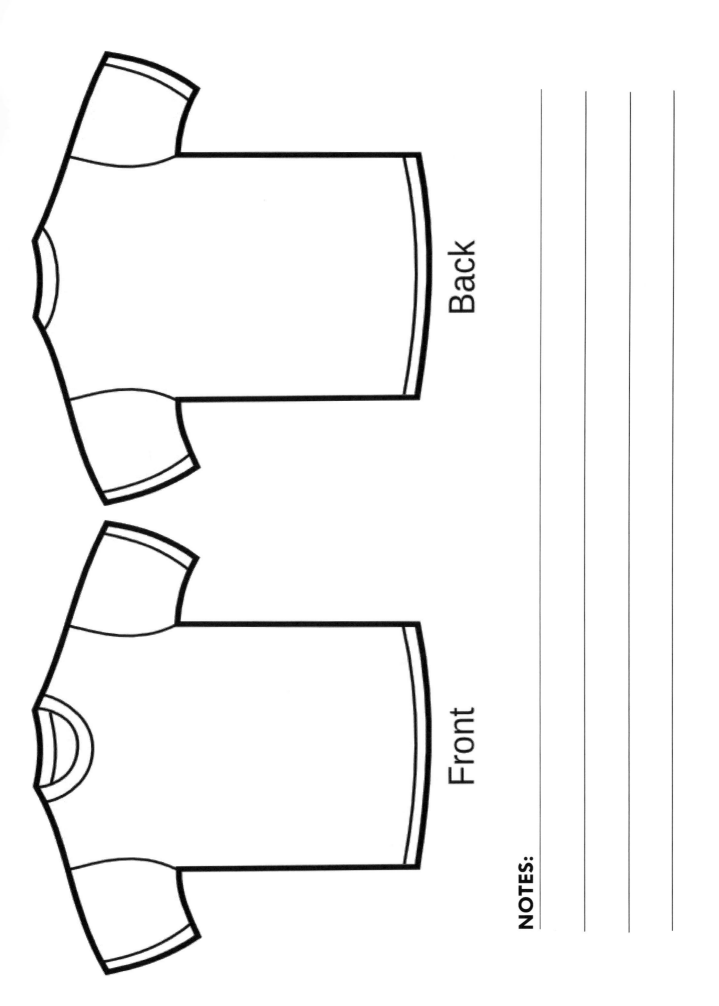

Back

Front

NOTES:

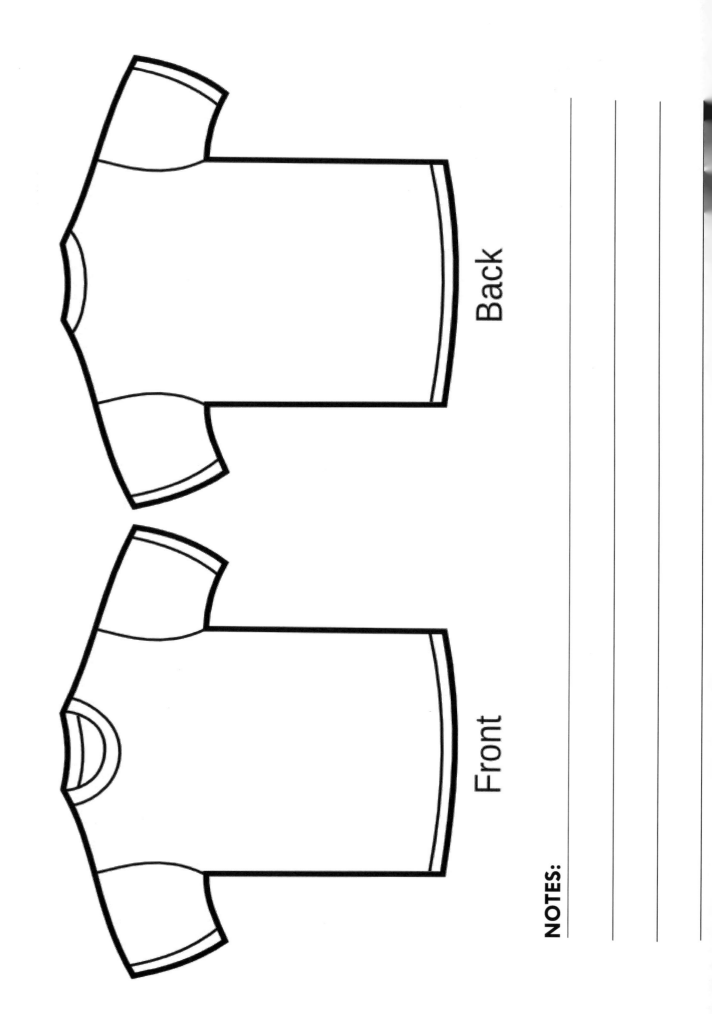

Back

Front

NOTES:

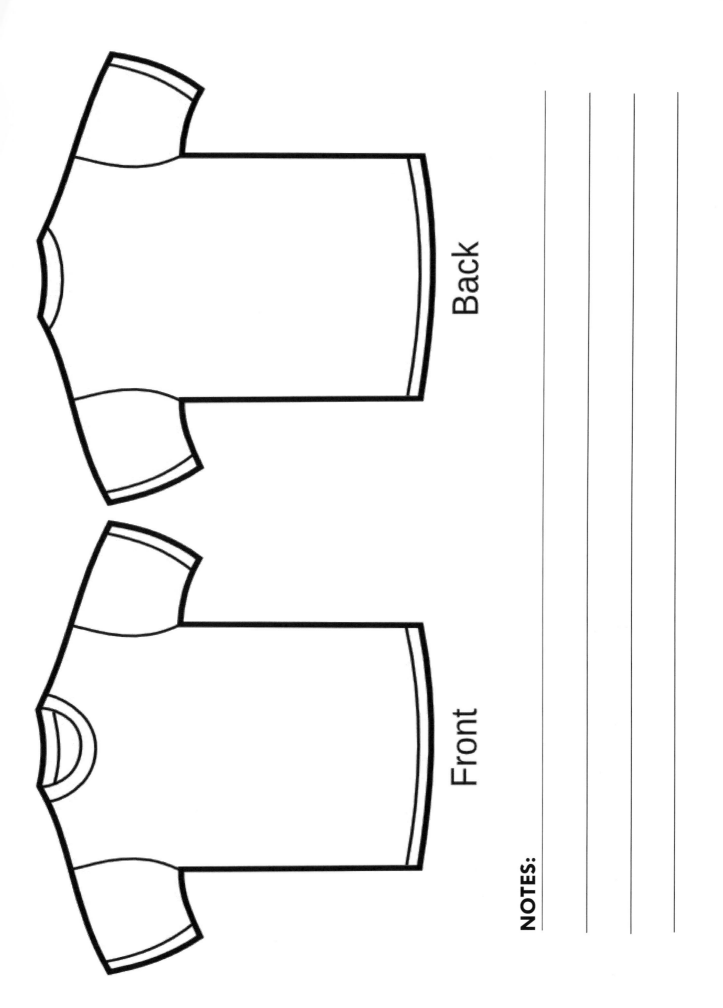

Back

Front

NOTES:

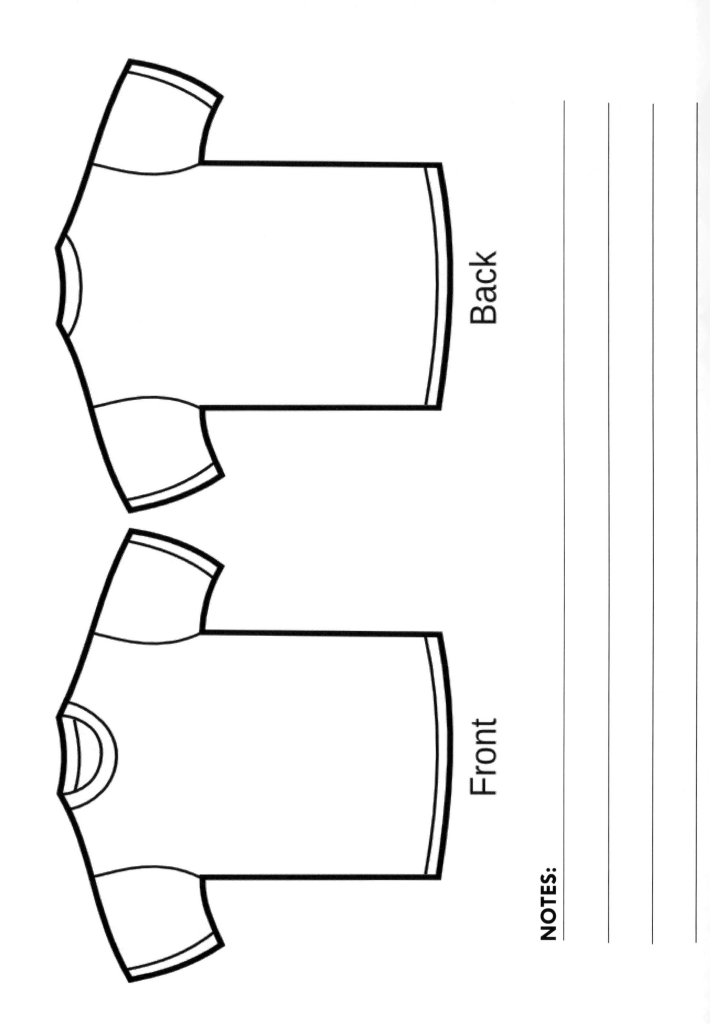

Back

Front

NOTES:

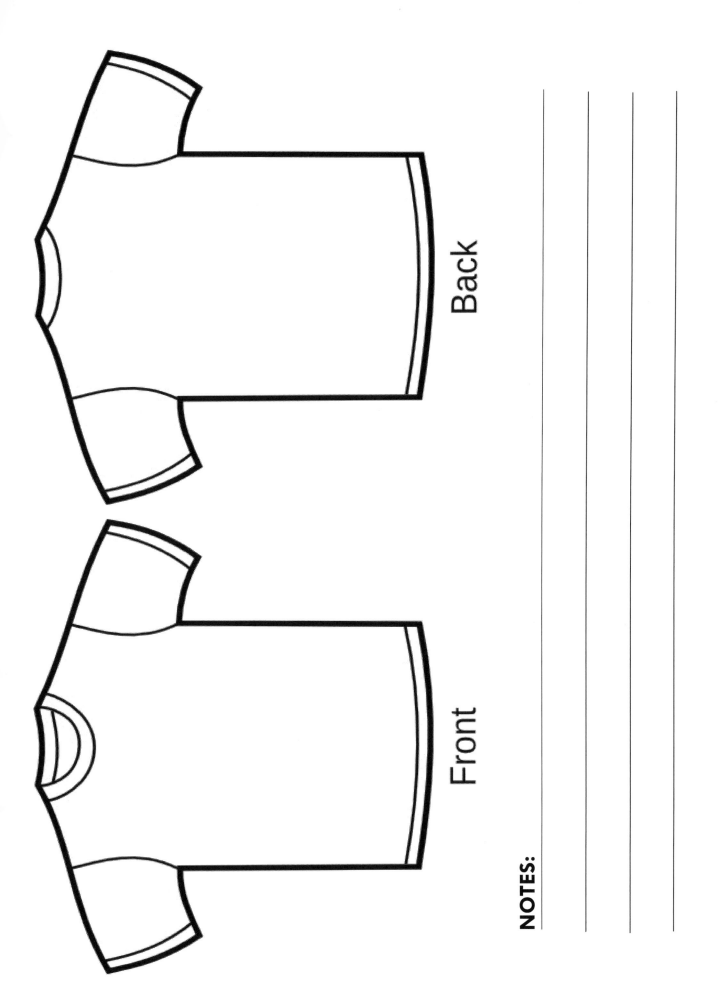

Back

Front

NOTES:

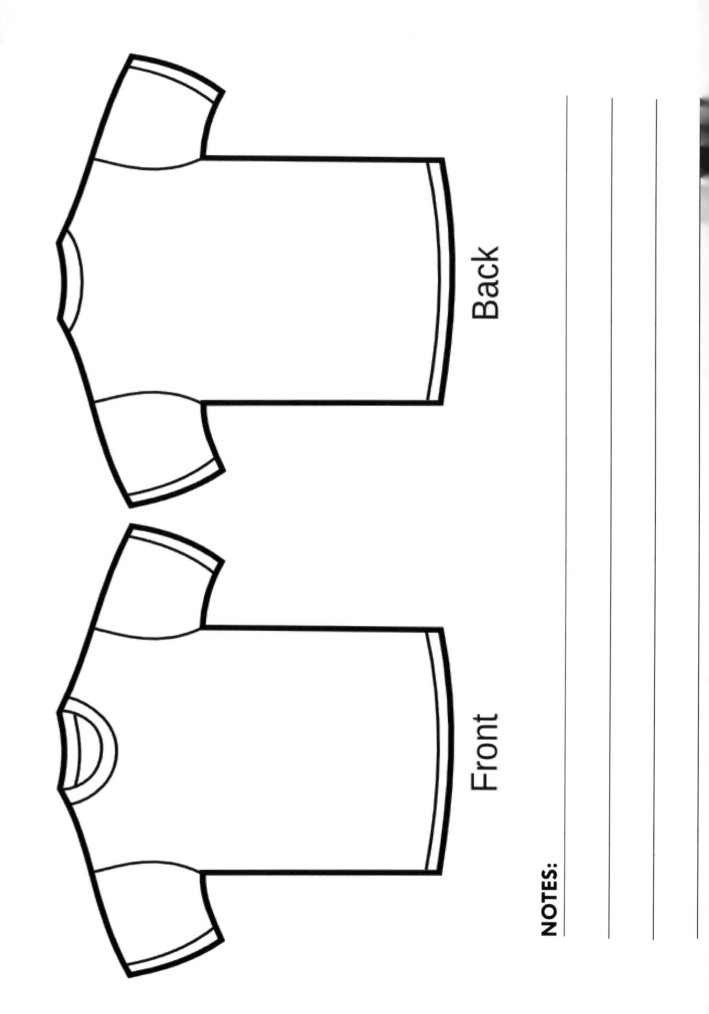

Back

Front

NOTES:

Made in the USA
Las Vegas, NV
08 May 2021